Building a Culture to Win

Expanding the Frontier of
Human Achievement

By Rob Ffield

Building a Culture to Win
Expanding the Frontier of Human Achievement

Copyright © 2014 Rob Ffield

Inspire On Purpose Publishing
Irving, Texas
(888) 403-2727
http://inspireonpurpose.com

The Platform Publisher™

Printed in the United States of America

Library of Congress Control Number: 2013944861

ISBN 10: 0982562241

ISBN 13: 978-0-9825622-4-6

*Use of released U.S. Navy imagery does not constitute product or organizational endorsement of any kind by the U.S. Navy.

Dedication

To the relentless innovators whose passion, free will and focus expand the frontier of human achievement.

.

TABLE OF CONTENTS

The Blue Angel Delta

Photo by Bernard Zee©

Flying Fast, Flying Tight

Our team of four Blue Angel F/A-18s is in full afterburner with our jet engines roaring at maximum power – about 450 mph, or more than twice as fast as the fastest NASCAR driver. We are accelerating rapidly only 25 feet above the ground.

Yet we are only 18 inches apart as we fly in our Diamond Formation.

With very little room for error, I make the calls in a rhythmic tone that keeps us all synchronized:

"Up we go . . . a little more pulllll."

The four of us simultaneously pull back on our control sticks in one fluid motion as we start our standard takeoff loop that will peak at an altitude of 8,000 feet above the ground. It is a perfect day for an air show practice, and we are going to go from the ground floor to more than five times the height of the Empire State Building in just seconds.

POW! Suddenly, we feel the unexpected punch of a thick cloud layer just as we begin our upward turn. The pre-flight weather forecast of a 10,000-foot ceiling was off by a few thousand feet. No matter how precisely you think you have gauged the weather, Mother Nature always has the last word.

Even in the best of conditions, executing and safely completing a looping maneuver directly from takeoff roll to the 200-foot bottom in a Diamond Formation is extremely difficult. Take away the ability to see the ground and difficult turns to almost impossible.

Traveling at such a remarkable speed, we all will have to pull our sticks back to exactly the same G-forces and use the exact throttle settings at the exact right time in the maneuver in order to exit the bottom of the clouds, still in our formation. If we are short a few Gs, we would find ourselves too steep and in danger of hitting the ground.

With the grace of a well-oiled machine developed over time in a culture of excellence, our team was able to face this one-in-a-million scenario and come out alive on the other side. We knew what to do and how to do it. And we did it, safely performing a challenging maneuver and returning to base without incident – but not without working up a bit of a sweat!

Our team was bigger than just my three wingmen and me. We had two Solo pilots in the air and a large ground team supporting us. They were just as motivated and connected to our success as the tight Diamond Formation pilots.

We were all part of a tradition. Nearly a century of Naval Aviation had cultivated successive improvements in organization, training, motivation, and leadership to match the exacting improvements in flying machines over the same period.

We were safe and successful because of a culture of excellence – an organizational outlook built around continual improvement and deep motivation, throughout the entire team.

"Visualize your team so well tuned, that not only can it execute the most difficult maneuvers in clear skies, but also when the environment is much more challenging."

U.S. Navy Photo

Tough Challenges Made a Culture of Excellence a Necessity

Not long after the Wright Brothers first took to the sky in 1903 in their wooden and canvas airplane, pioneer naval aviators began to attempt the *then* impossible – taking off and landing on ships at sea.

Much of the success of World War I was attributed to those early pioneers of Naval Aviation. The necessity and inherent danger of naval flight bred an organizational culture of excellence that began during that war, and was taken to the limit in combat during World War II. Every member of the team knew what was on the line if they failed – lives would be lost.

As Naval Aviation advanced, powerful steam catapults were developed in the mid-1950s to launch heavier and more powerful jet aircraft – from zero to 160 knots in seconds. This development only increased the need for exacting teamwork and flawless flight skills.

Today, a catapult launch, or CATSHOT, is perhaps the most intense experience in aviation – and the first indicator of a mission's success.

The CATSHOT – which takes only seconds – represents the transition point from the planning and preparation phase of a mission to the actual mission execution phase. It is here that we see the culmination of all of our plans put into motion. It is here that we see our momentum in play. It is here that we see our plans tested against reality.

In flight, as in business, you must begin with thorough and methodical pre-mission planning. Everything related to the goals of your mission must be planned, briefed, and reviewed. Before you can take your CATSHOT, you must make sure you have a precise alignment of all of your crew members, and of all of the key technical systems.

Once the CATSHOT is made, your aircraft – or project or company or team – is in motion, and the execution of your plan begins. The execution of your plan is the most exciting part of the process. However, we will learn in this book that the importance of having a plan to land and a plan to debrief are key to your continued success.

If you want your team to continue to improve and have lifelong success, each mission – or project – must be assessed for both its successes and its failures. Capturing lessons learned and sharing them with the team helps you to adjust goals and tactics in real time, allowing you to improve the execution of future missions and improve your bottom line.

If you want your company, or team, to fly fast and tight like the Blue Angels do in the Diamond Formation, you must develop an infinite loop, which begins with planning. Then in execution, valuable lessons are learned, and during the debriefing improvements are developed. The cycle starts over again by deliberately planning for the next execution, and around again and again. I will help you develop the tools to create such an organization based on the lessons that I learned flying the skies with the Blue Angels and TOPGUN.

How to Use this Book

This book focuses on giving you the sense of what it is like to actually be there with some of the world's highest performing teams. I will draw lessons from my experience with the Blue Angels and the U.S. Navy Fighter Weapons School, better known as TOPGUN. We will also look to top performing organizations such as Apple, Starbucks and the 1980 U.S. Olympic ice hockey team.

As I walk you through each step in the process for developing a top performing organization, I will offer a visualization exercise. Visualization is a key skill that will help move your plan forward. You and your team must be able to imagine and experience the risk and the rewards of achieving excellence.

To learn the most from the sometimes-hair-raising lessons, you will need to open your mind and place yourself in the moment. Experiencing the physical environment and personal interactions as if they were happening in real time is a very important aspect of rising toward success. Developing this one skill – visualization – personally and within your team will help take you to new heights.

True visualization will help you successfully execute events in a world-class manner, because it ingrains the picture of success – whatever that means to you and your team – into your subconscious. You should feel as though you have actually lived through each scenario.

Just as world-class athletes visualize themselves winning prior to an actual competition, you will be able to visualize the inner workings of a world-class organization. You can then use your visualization experience to build your own culture to win.

Chair flying is a very important component of the Blue Angels' training. The Blues literally sit in office chairs, close their eyes and assume the position they would in their F/A-18s—including grabbing a make-believe control stick and throttle with their hands while pressing on imaginary rudder pedals with their feet. Therefore, at the end of each chapter, we will offer you a similar opportunity to chair fly the concepts you have just read.

What this book is: This book is a portal for you to gain the experience few have had – to actually be part of a world-class organization. It gives you the sense and experience without actually being there, and helps you feel what it is like to succeed.

The concepts apply to any type of organization, whether you work in a family business, for a community group, or in a Fortune 500 company. They also apply to subcultures. It works if you are starting an organization, merging organizations, or simply trying to improve the culture of an existing organization.

What this book is not: This is not a textbook. A purely academic study of business will not promote the understanding of the real secret to organizational success.

Yes, budgets should balance, and investments of time and money should be made. However, those organizations that take off from the pack are those whose leaders understand the importance of looking beyond the numbers. They recognize that everyone in the organization should understand what it feels like to succeed, and then create a culture to make it a reality.

The examples in this book are derived from hard-core, real-world examples where the consequences of not succeeding can be disastrous in terms of life and/or treasure.

How these lessons apply to you: The highly structured environment of the U.S. military can appear daunting to civilians. You may wonder if a book full of military examples can apply to your organization, business, or sports team with their more lax structure. In addition, the military uses a non-negotiable pay scale with its bonus structure based primarily on retention and on hazard pay — not performance.

Let me assure you that, while the U.S. military uses a hierarchical structure and few financial incentives, it promotes and provides substantial room for individual free will and understands the importance of non-monetary incentives. All organizations, whether in the private sector or military, must offer more than just money.

Just as if we were in the air, the key to success in the military and in business is balance — and the never-ending need to continually correct for atmospheric conditions.

The best organizational cultures are able to align people's passions while also promoting agility and resilience by using free will to anticipate, innovate, and adapt as necessary. These organizations have missions that are easily understood by their employees, customers, vendors, shareholders and all other stakeholders. By focusing all of their stakeholders on their missions – and not merely the bottom lines – these world-class organizations accelerate past their competition and the money follows.

If you want to win, do not focus on just winning. Focus on creating the culture of excellence that will help you win! I will explain in Chapter 1 how bringing all of the pieces of a culture of excellence together means creating a Performance Triad built on passion, free will, and focus of the individual and the team.

*"Team cultures that naturally seek the perfect balance of passion,
free will and focus are consistent winners no matter how
challenging the environment and how complex the mission!"*

U.S. Navy Photo Taken By MC1 Johnnie Robbins, USN

Section 1:

Ready the Team -

Preparing for the CATSHOT

Strapped in solo but not alone, I sat on the deck of the USS Coral Sea behind the controls of an F/A-18 Hornet. It weighed in at about 50,000 pounds fully loaded and was worth a cool $35 million. And they put it in the hands of a 24-year-old on his first real world alert launch.

Soviet Bear Bombers were transiting through our airspace at night and I had been given the word to "launch the alert," just 15 minutes earlier.

Flight ops had been complete for the day and the ship was heading north for Norfolk from the Cuban operating area at the completion of our workups for deployment. I had been relaxing that evening with my squadron mates in the ship's forecastle. In keeping with Navy tradition, we were participating in skits and award ceremonies at the end of our operational sea period.

It was my time to stand alert 60, which was the lowest level of alert and the least likely to launch. However, that night, the bombers unexpectedly turned in our direction. Next thing I knew, I went from very comfortable social surroundings dressed in my non-flying khaki uniform, to being moments away from a launch into a very dark night from a catapult that would shoot me from zero to 150 knots in as little as two seconds, wearing full combat gear.

This was the CATSHOT, the moment that we went from planning to execution of our mission.

Trust. That was all that stood between disaster and me. I say I was not alone because I knew that a ground crew of two plane captains had checked every inch of my craft, 170-plus individuals in the maintenance department had the F/A-18 Hornet in tip-top mechanical shape, and the Air Boss in the control tower and the Flight Deck Handler made sure our multi-million-dollar machines missed each other, even if only by inches.

I had to trust that I was working with the best team in the business, and they would not let me down. The precision and focus needed in preparation to launch is incredible and the actual CATSHOT itself puts forces on your body and senses that are matched nowhere.

The list of things that can go wrong is endless.

From the moment you step on the flight deck to preflight your aircraft, you are in significant danger. You have to navigate through a maze of hot exhaust gases from turning jet engines and endure incredible noise and body-piercing vibration as pilots select full afterburner for takeoff just a few feet away. You are constantly exposed to a cocktail of oil-impregnated catapult steam, heat, sea spray, and heavy winds, and the entire path to your aircraft is a maze of hazards including turning propellers, rotor blades, refueling hoses, spilled oil, grease and hydraulic fluid, sharp metal, and explosive ordnance.

It is the world's most dynamic and dangerous environment to work in during the daytime and becomes even more dangerous at night.

However, the men and women who have worked and operated from the flight deck of a U.S. Navy aircraft carrier will tell you that this seemingly chaotic environment is actually one of the most finely tuned, well-choreographed operations ever developed.

What may seem like a menagerie of individuals wearing different color jerseys randomly moving around the deck is, in fact, a group of motivated individuals carrying out their very specific responsibilities in a highly coordinated and synergistic fashion.

It is the Naval Aviation culture that enables individuals, many as young as 18 years old, to successfully launch billions of dollars of aircraft in a safe, yet expeditious, manner. As you are reading this, they are performing their missions flawlessly around the globe in the most demanding environmental conditions.

Like Navy aircrew going into combat, a business or team must be prepared to launch on its mission. The better the culture of preparation is, the more consistent success will be.

Let's begin.

"Team selection and placement – cultures of excellence make this their highest priority."

U.S. Navy Photo Taken By MC2 Jen Blake

Chapter 1:
The Performance Triad™

Straight Up into the Clouds: How Passion, Free Will and Focus Enable the Impossible

Worldclass teams have a unique aura and mystique that people can feel the moment they come into contact with them.

Those inside the organization are excited to be there; they know they are part of something special. The passion for what they do fuels a constant effort to always improve and innovate. They are living in a culture of excellence where the success of an individual or department raises the performance of the entire organization.

Those on the outside see an unstoppable team exuding confidence in everything they do. Outsiders cannot always put their finger on why, but they feel a desire to be around them, to work with them. The team's enthusiasm is contagious.

I have been lucky enough to be part of two world-class teams with international reputations for excellence – the Blue Angels and the U.S. Navy Fighter Weapons School, better known as TOPGUN. My experience with these two organizations taught me that they had three overarching factors needed for their success – *The Performance Triad*:

Passion. Each team member had a passion for the organization. Passion is the fuel that drives individuals to achieve beyond what is normally considered humanly possible. Passion is what makes team members live, eat and breathe the organization, thus creating momentum.

Free will. Free will may seem to be counterintuitive as a key teamwork skill. Yet, when properly harnessed, it serves as the oxygen for the fire fueled by passion. Free will stokes the fire of innovation and fuels continuous improvement. The more free will, the hotter the flames burn.

Focus. Focus brings heat to the fire. Focus is what hones the momentum created by your team's passion and harnesses the direction of the team members' free will.

Without fuel, oxygen and heat, you will produce no flame. Likewise, letting any leg of The Performance Triad fall away – passion, free will or focus – will not produce a world-class organization.

When the elements of The Performance Triad are present in the proper balance, a team will be functioning at its optimal level. Just as a fire must be continuously managed to produce the best flame, an organization must always be adjusted to produce the best results.

Your goal is to build an organizational culture where the proper equilibrium between the three elements becomes self-seeking – the culture finds the best balance with little intervention and adjusts as necessary for changing conditions.

Truly world-class teams have cultures that naturally seek optimal equilibrium between passion, free will and focus.

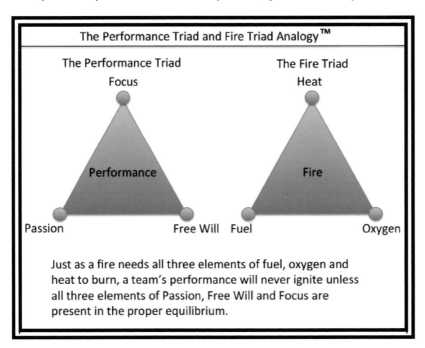

Passion, Free Will and Focus Spark the Rebirth of a Squadron

In the fall of 1990, the Navy was transitioning a large portion of its aircraft carrier-based aircrafts from the A-7

Corsair attack aircraft to the new F/A-18 Hornet Strike Fighter aircraft. Due to that transition, Attack Squadron 105 (VA-105), based in Naval Air Station Cecil Field Florida, was slated for decommissioning.

The squadron known as the "Gunslingers" divested itself of most of its key assets including many pilots and maintenance personnel. The remaining pilots flew minimal hours and prepared their old A-7s to be mothballed.

In mid-January 1991, President George H.W. Bush ordered the start of Operation Desert Storm to liberate Kuwait after Saddam Hussein's Iraqi forces invaded. The U.S. military's plans changed almost overnight, as the massive deployment of nearly all combat-ready squadrons began.

The almost-decommissioned VA-105 Gunslingers would not be one of them.

As the rest of the naval squadrons began their prep for deployment, the Navy realized it needed a place to send the new F/A-18 Hornets rolling off the factory floor. As a result, the Gunslinger's decommissioning was halted, and its designation was changed to Strike Fighter Squadron 105 (VFA-105) as it began receiving the brand new Hornets.

When I arrived at the VFA-105, we had new jets and a few great people, but not much else. It was time to rebuild.

The partial decommissioning process had taken its toll. The Gunslingers went from being one of the nation's premier squadrons in the A-7 days, to one that was struggling and unfocused. It was time to kick The Performance Triad into high gear.

An Amazing Transformation

We had a great Commanding Officer and Executive Officer who allowed the Gunslinger Department Heads, including me, to use our initiative – our free will – to develop a vision of what was possible for the squadron.

My passion for flight operations, along with the ability of my fellow department heads to tap into the passion and free will of the officers and sailors under their charge, led us to the goal of out-planning, out-training, and out-flying all the other squadrons on our base.

We focused on the task at hand – combat readiness – by dropping more practice ordnance, shooting more bullets, and flying more hours than any other squadron. We would execute with meaning, with the emphasis on "deliberate practice," more than ever before. We aimed to be innovative in how we employed the new aircraft and how we organized the effort of the team.

We worked to reignite the passion of our team – extracting the most from every training evolution and developing a culture that enhanced the capabilities of every junior officer and every one of our support personnel.

For pilots, pre-flight briefs and post-flight debriefs were extensive and thorough. Everything we did was oriented toward how we could do things better. The maintenance team focused with equal passion and began to achieve sortie completion rates that were unheard of.

We shared our passion and worked to encourage the same feeling in others. Pretty soon, the passion began to spread – more individuals were willing to exercise their free will in innovation. The whole team became motivated.

As a result, tangible evidence of improvement appeared at all levels in the work of pilots, maintenance crew, and administrative personnel. Individuals were now taking initiative on their own to improve upon systems, ideas and techniques.

For example, we raised enough money to be the first squadron to have our own gym in our squadron spaces. This gave pilots more opportunity in their busy schedule to stay in peak physical condition. We played harder. We worked smarter. And we enjoyed every moment.

It was an awesome time to be a Gunslinger!

Writing Our Story

We not only worked hard and tried new things; we focused on best practices and created standard procedures that everyone followed. We began to develop our story – a combination of lore, incidents, and practices – that we shared and repeated to others.

Documenting the squadron's story created an expectation. When anyone joined the squadron, they already knew they were now part of a culture of excellence – they were expected to uphold those ideals to be part of the team.

Every winning organization develops a legacy of achievements that come together to tell its story. This legacy focuses team members on accomplishments and standards, attracting others who are motivated to add their own chapters. It is a key part of making the Triad sustainable.

In addition, putting your story on paper helps your team – as well as those who are watching your team – better visualize what it is like to be a winner. Visualization of what success looks like is key to getting you and your team to the same place at the same time.

Over time, organizations develop mystiques, culture with which all members of the team, new and old, can identify – they have the same vision of success. Individually, they become part of the story; the legacy. This motivates them to take part and to do what it takes to maintain the high levels of innovation and execution necessary to consistently perform at the world-class level.

The Triad in Business

My experience with The Performance Triad in these military teams can be seen reflected in the success stories of teams in private business and sports.

- Apple Computers – Steve Jobs, the innovative, no-compromise leader of Apple, consistently focused on quality and function in how he designed and built Apple's products. He made sure they encompassed excellence on every conceivable level, from external packaging to the smallest detail of interior construction. When Steve Jobs was forced out as the Apple CEO in 1985, his culture of excellence went with him and Apple suffered. Upon his return, Jobs was able to re-establish the culture by infusing his passion for constant improvement, harnessing the free will of his employees that led to innovations, and focusing the company on what it does best – deliver innovative, personal consumer electronics. He then took steps to make the culture stick upon his eventual absence.

- Starbucks – Howard Schultz, CEO of Starbucks, took a cheap commodity – coffee – and turned it into an experience. He demonstrated that customers would pay for a superior coffee paired with a high-quality customer experience. Schultz's passion for coffee and customer service was contagious. Starbucks grew seemingly without effort, so Schultz felt he could step away from the day-to-day management. However, the company soon lost its focus during a quick expansion. Schultz returned to re-focus the organization around a team of individuals who shared his passion and his focus. He let go those who did not. Starbucks also learned to harness the passion and free will of its customers and staff by creating a forum for bringing forth product ideas that the company tests for use in its stores.

- 1980 U.S. Olympic Ice Hockey Team – Twenty young American men from differing backgrounds and only eight-months of training performed "The Miracle on Ice" by defeating the much more experienced Soviet Olympic Ice Hockey team at the 1980 Olympics. USA coach Herb Brooks hand-selected the team, taking careful stock of their skating and stick skills. As legend has it, he was obsessed with putting together a team, not just a group of individuals. Therefore, he also evaluated each player's personal drive to contribute to the team as a whole. Brooks refocused the team members' loyalties from their college teams to Team USA. He built their passion around the honor of playing for their country, not for themselves. With this new focus, Brooks was able to harness the players' passions that allowed them the freedom, or free will, to use their skills the best way they saw fit.

Each of these examples of world-class organizations needs little explanation, because we all know their story. Their exuberance for their professions is palpable. They are surrounded by a contagious sense of mastery, and their laser-like focus on efficient execution of the smallest details makes the difficult look easy. They consistently deliver breathtaking performances.

People want to be with winners, and mutual support among and across teams is a vital factor in resilience over time.

If you look inside those teams, you will find passion, free will and focus all hard at work.

Points to Remember

1. ***Passion*** is the fuel that motivates individuals and groups to put in maximum effort.

2. ***Free will*** is the oxygen that enables innovation and a continuous search for mastery.

3. ***Focus*** concentrates both passion and free will to create enough heat to ignite a fire.

4. A balanced ***Performance Triad*** consisting of passion, free will, and focus is necessary to maximize output.

5. ***Visualization*** is key to taking your team or organization to the next level. All team members must be able to see what success is and work together to achieve it.

Chair Flying Exercise

Think back to my example of the fast and tight Blue Angel Diamond Formation, and how we were headed upward into the sky in perfect synchronicity when – POW! – we were hit with an unexpected, blinding cloud layer.

- What did success look like to us? Safely completing the loop without hitting the ground.

- What were our high-risk factors? Our high rate of speed, the closeness of our formation.

- What were our obstacles? Our inability to see each other or the ground.

- What did we do? We stuck to the plan as if the obstacle was not there, and trusted each other to execute as we had many times before and pull out the formation safely above the ground.

Put yourself in the cockpit of the Blue Angel jet leading a perfect Diamond Formation.

Think about the preparation, teamwork, and communication needed to perform a loop in very close formation, starting very close to the ground and successfully completing that loop at the same height above the ground – all at 450 Knots. Think about the gorgeous blue skies and being able to see the smiles of your fellow pilots.

Now visualize doing it when you cannot see the ground, and you are going straight down in the clouds with no reference to the earth. You can barely see your fellow pilots, yet you know they are inches away. How do you hope the team reacts?

Now think about your own organization, team or business. What are some of the most difficult processes you must perform with precision every time? If you could not be there with your team members while they performed that process, what do you hope they all do? Do you trust them to do that?

Does your team have the passion, free will, and focus to continually seek ways to improve or are they satisfied with the status quo? Close your eyes and visualize how your team would complete that difficult process in perfect harmony. What is each team member doing individually? How is each team member interacting with the others?

Write down your thoughts and share them with your team. Get their feedback on why the process works or would not work. Put some of the changes into place, then debrief after the process has been completed a few times with the changes.

Repeat this process and take note of the changes in both the process and in your team. Work with them to visualize what success would look like. Make sure you all have the same vision. Begin to assess team members on their engagement (passion) in the new visualization process (focus) and their willingness to contribute and offer their ideas and concerns (free will).

Managers can introduce The Performance Triad to the company, and create an atmosphere for it to ignite. However, employees must embrace the Triad for its benefits to permeate the organization. Close your eyes and imagine what that looks like, then ask yourself what you can do to engage your employees in the same vision.

"Cultures of excellence naturally attract and select Relentless Innovators who are always seeking improvement and perfection even in the most simple tasks."

U.S. Navy Photo

Chapter 2:

The Value of Relentless Innovators

Reinventing TOPGUN

It was a bright sunny day in June 1988 in San Diego when I walked into the front door of the U.S. Navy Fighter Weapons School, better known in the military as TOPGUN. It was my first of two tours as an air combat instructor. I was 29 years old, single and eager to begin training with this elite squadron made famous just two years earlier in the blockbuster movie, "Top Gun."

The Navy's then-20-year-old process of selecting and training its fighter pilots, as well as its policy to immediately send them right back to their fleet squadrons, remained unchanged since the program's inception. That process made sense during the Vietnam conflict, as the Navy needed to get the best tactics back to the guys in the fight as quickly as possible — lives were at stake.

With all that publicity and fanfare surrounding the TOPGUN program at this time, I was sure that the tried-and-true method of training the best fighter pilots in the world and turning them into instructors was as good as it could get.

I was wrong.

The tactical landscape had changed dramatically in sophistication and capability. As before, we still needed pilots who had the eye of a tiger in the air-to-air combat arena. However, we also needed our pilots to have a highly technical understanding of their weapons system, as well as the teaching skills to coach others on how to successfully defeat the enemy. Additionally, the list of threat weapons systems that they had to know, equally as well as their own, was only increasing every day in both lethality and proliferation.

We needed to raise the level of performance for the best fighter pilots in the world – much, much higher.

Prompted by research into U.S. Air Force and Marine air combat training programs and by our own intuition that we could find ways to train our combat aviators better, my fellow TOPGUN instructors and I began to formulate a new training methodology. It was bold. It was very different. And it would require significant changes in the manning and equipping of TOPGUN and the fleet squadrons.

We knew that our new, improved training would elevate the combat readiness of the entire Naval Aviation community when it was complete. However, we also knew that we were in for a challenge as this was a change in status quo from a system that seemed to be working well and that was glorified in the movies. The changes would require shifting millions of dollars of assets as we fundamentally reorganized how TOPGUN students would be equipped to complete the course and how these students were later assigned their duties.

As expected, our first proposals to those effected organizations were met with significant resistance. We heard all of the standard *status quo* defense arguments: "Why change something that is not broken?" "It will cost more in the long run." "The Fleet squadrons won't support this."

Despite clear evidence from our research and planning that we had to change, the project continued to meet with resistance.

Yet, from that point forward, a long list of distinguished fellow TOPGUN instructors became Relentless Innovators – they not only had great ideas, but also led the charge for the execution of those ideas. True innovators do not simply toss out ideas; they actually work to make them happen.

These Relentless Innovators ignored the naysayers and forged ahead to create the Navy's new Air Combat

Training Continuum (ACTC) and TOPGUN's new Strike Fighter Weapons and Tactics Instructor (SFWTI) course. They understood the words spoken by one of our nations' first Relentless Innovators, Henry Ford:

> *"Enthusiasm is the yeast that makes your hopes shine to the stars. Vision without execution is just hallucination."*

Despite our powerful drive and strong resolve, our new training program was still in jeopardy five years later when I returned for my second tour at TOPGUN. We knew we would have to be relentlessly persistent if we were to do what we knew was right and to overcome our critics.

Fast forward to today: The ACTC and SFWTI programs are heralded as the cutting-edge in air combat training. Other communities within the Navy and other services have modeled programs in a similar fashion. Amazingly, many of the former naysayers are now the biggest proponents.

Without the dedication of our Relentless Innovators, the TOPGUN changes would never have taken place. This incredible group of dedicated men and women showed what a determined, committed group could do. They made the Navy more effective in combat, and our nation is better for it.

The reinvention of TOPGUN remains one of my best examples of what it takes to challenge organizational status quo and win. It highlights the importance of having a system that recruits and promotes Relentless Innovators who will relentlessly pursue organizational improvements.

Relentless Innovators Continually Strengthen and Reinvent their Organizations

So, who are the Relentless Innovators? They are people who can think on their feet and have a drive to innovate. They see "No" as a challenge to navigate, not a roadblock to avoid.

We have all seen people work their way up in an organization simply by biding their time and not making mistakes. They do not improve anything along the way. They are the maintainers of the *status quo*.

These caretakers, who can be found at every level of an organization, rarely leave an organization much better than it was when they started. They do their jobs, but they do not do much more. They do not innovate.

In contrast to caretakers, Relentless Innovators constantly build and innovate. They are not bound solely by *status quo* procedures and checklists to determine what needs to be done. While caretakers may be good people who are efficient at executing their responsibilities as described, they lack the added motivation, or maybe even the guts, to improve their organizations.

Therefore, whether you are hiring from outside or promoting from within, a key attribute of a culture of excellence is implementing a hiring system that will attract a solid core of Relentless Innovator candidates.

When you are a fighter pilot – especially when you are part of the Blue Angels or TOPGUN – playing as a team isn't just a slogan. Your life is literally in the hands of your fellow naval aviators. A wrong move could easily create a tragedy. With that constant reality, everyone wants to know they are working with the best and that those people have the drive to always search for improvement, and the conviction to put the team and executing the plan ahead of themselves.

The Process and Culture of Selecting a Team

TOPGUN and the Blue Angels have the luxury of being able to observe candidates over a period of time so they really get to know them well. This also allows both organizations to look into not only qualifications and experience that would demonstrate their aptitude for being a Relentless Innovator, but also the more subtle, yet critical, attributes such as chemistry and core values which are covered in the next chapter.

As an example, the Blue Angels has developed a very deliberate seven-month process that begins in the off-season in December with a Navy-wide solicitation for applications. The process ends in June when a group of seven to ten finalists is brought to Pensacola, FL, for formal interviews and eventual selection.

The Blues often get 50-70 applications for just two to three pilot slots. How they cull through them is very strategic. Formal interviews are important, but it is the process between December and June the team finds most critical in the selection process.

During that time, applicants are encouraged to get to know more about the team by attending pre-show briefings and also post-show public commitments each weekend. This is how the Blues can get to really know each candidate, who they are, and what they are all about.

It is important to note that there is no flying evaluation for the pilots. Their expertise in that area is well-documented through the Navy training system.

The team is looking beyond those metrics for the more subtle attributes found in chemistry and core values. It is also important to note that the entire team, from officer to enlisted, is involved in getting to know candidates, not just the other F/A-18 demonstration pilots. Similarly, the entire officer core is involved in the final interviews and selection deliberations, which take several days. They are brutal because the stakes are so high.

The support team members are also selected in a similar fashion and the process is conducted exclusively by the team themselves with no outside intervention from the Navy Flag Officers, other than some very basic guidelines on the candidates future potential as a Naval Officer.

This method is time-tested and is a critical element of the Blue Angel culture of excellence.

Like the Blues, world-class organizations develop cultures that go beyond assessing just the critical expertise and technical skills needed for a particular position. Those skills are only the beginning.

Leaders of world-class organizations want to know if the prospective team members can speak and communicate well. They want to know if the candidates have a passion for the job and for doing it right. They want people they can develop into leaders, people who are Relentless Innovators, people who understand that every program and process can be improved.

In my capacity as the Blue Angel's Commanding Officer and lead pilot, or "Boss," the process of picking team members was challenging – as important in many ways as the toughest aspects of flying. It is meticulous and time-consuming, but always worth the effort. It was a process I learned to never short-change. It would not be fair to me, or the organization, to have the wrong person join our team.

Observations Into the Nature of Top Team Performers

We have talked about the importance of passion and focus in selecting new team members for high-performance teams. My decades of experience selecting and observing pilots for the Navy's elite organizations has shown me that there is a direct correlation between documented performance during initial flight training and how quickly a pilot masters more advanced skills, such as the skills needed to perform precision flight demonstrations, dogfighting skills, and landing on an aircraft carrier.

I have found many of these fast learners are Relentless Innovators by nature. They are also fun people to be around!

The same is true of my experience in business. Some people are slower learners that may catch on eventually, but for high-level teams, you need fast learners who adapt and innovate quickly.

Again, we see a theme in common with the "reinventing TOPGUN" story: choose people who are flexible and adaptable and who have a strong passion for learning, improvement, innovation and persistence. They have fun doing these activities, which is why they are so good.

In general, it is useful to get insight into how quickly a team member can learn. For instance, a TOPGUN instructor could likely take a good college athlete with no flying experience and turn him into a good fighter pilot simply based on his passion for competition, work ethic, and how quickly he adapted and tackled new challenges in the past.

Attitude matters. Spirit and drive propel these individuals to perform beyond their peers. These are the people who I want on my team.

Finding Relentless Innovators for Business

From my experience in the Navy and also advising large fortune 100 companies, only a small percentage of people are Relentless Innovators. The entrepreneurial candidates are who really make substantial contributions and innovations to an organization. Most of the other people are caretakers.

In putting together a team to win, emphasis must be on selecting more Relentless Innovators and putting them in the right roles. Sure, you need technical experts for specific areas, but these people may or may not be Relentless Innovators. Indeed, Relentless Innovators will sometimes execute even better without any prior experience as they quickly outpace the so-called "experts."

It boils down to whether or not a candidate has a go-for-it attitude and can learn and reboot quickly to execute at a world-class level and make things happen.

So how do you determine one's propensity to be a Relentless Innovator?

First, use the direct approach and ask them to describe their history of innovation – from idea through execution. Really take the time to get to know the individual and ask for specifics. You will find out quickly how driven and sincere they are at putting the organization ahead of themselves.

Next, I found true character references are vital – the more in-depth, the better. Written references alone are almost worthless. They must be verified with probing questions. If you cannot directly observe a candidate in action yourself, discussing someone's past performance with former colleagues in a confidential, non-attribution setting is the next-best option.

Whether promoting from within or hiring from outside, the most important question in determining your job candidate's expertise is: "What is his/her track record of innovation from idea to execution?"

Another indicator to consider is the candidate's passion. Passion is more than just a person's field of expertise or interest. Passion is, in the big picture, about the will to do a job – any job you give them – to the best of their ability and have fun doing it.

Again, the number one consideration in all of this is their track record. Have they, in their past roles, shown themselves to be passionate about executing tasks and accomplishing them to the best of their ability, regardless of the role's prestige? If so, they are Relentless Innovators.

They are the people you want on your team.

Finally, the elements of team chemistry and core values must be considered. When you have the luxury of being able to select from a large group of qualified candidates, these considerations become the tiebreakers. These elements are of such great importance that the next chapter is dedicated to exploring them further.

Raising Your Average

The Blue Angels and TOPGUN hiring experiences were fun.

The same was true when I was the executive officer running a four-star general's staff. The team and staff members had a rewarding experience really getting to know the new job candidates.

They enthusiastically participated. Not only did they want to find the right person to complement the team, but they also learned a great deal with each round of interviews. Many of the individuals we did not select became great friends, as well as great professional contacts and colleagues, due to our spirited approach to hiring.

Our mindset went beyond just hiring great people. Our mindset was focused on finding the *right* great people.

When you are intent on building a culture of excellence, it is important to "raise your averages" in finding the best innovators. You will have to customize an approach that works for you – the "how." The "what" should be a focus on providing clear job descriptions, identifying questionable claims on résumés, and uncovering more accurate information about a job candidate through traditional methods.

Even if you cannot do exactly what we were able to do in selecting Blue Angel pilots and instructors, you can and should use every tool at your disposal to locate and select top performers - Relentless Innovators. They will be key to creating a culture of excellence.

Your Relentless Innovators will help you recruit other Relentless Innovators, and they will even influence people in your organization who may not naturally tend to be

Relentless Innovators. They, too, will become excited and passionate – and they will start to contribute at a higher level.

Ultimately, once you have established an organization of Relentless Innovators, it naturally attracts more of the same who identify and want to be associated with a world-class team. You know you are world class when the process is fun, and you have Relentless Innovators knocking at your door.

Points to Remember

1. The world's best teams have cultures that attract, hire and retain Relentless Innovators. They not only provide the idea, but also execute to make sure the idea becomes reality.

2. Relentless Innovators are the entrepreneurs within an organization who make substantial contributions to innovation, improvement, and excellence in execution.

3. Cultures of excellence make the hiring process a learning experience that is exciting and fun for all involved, and make it an all-hands responsibility.

Chair Flying Exercise

Visualize the six-month process the Blue Angels use to select team members. Imagine culling through stacks of applications – every one of them highly qualified. Think about what Blue Angels pilots do – fly expensive, fast machines very close together while dynamically maneuvering through the sky. The situation is exhilarating, but could be terrifying, and even fatal, if done incorrectly.

What do you think is harder for us to determine from those applications – flying skills or the ability to stay calm under pressure? Flying skills are easily documented.

What are some of the characteristics you think we need to see from untested, potential team members? Someone who is relentless in finding ways to be even better than the best, who is also willing to implement those changes.

Now think about your organization. Do you have an in-depth understanding of the type of individual you want to hire – beyond the required expertise and experience? What characteristics beyond technical expertise do you envision your perfect employee possessing?

What process do you have in place to ascertain if they have these characteristics? Do you even have such a process?

If your organization had a culture that saw the hiring process as an all-hands effort, not just left to the human resources department, but as a team-wide responsibility – who would you want on that team? How would you make the process something to look forward to doing?

Now visualize your organization with a culture that naturally attracts Relentless Innovators. You have an endless stream of applicants every time a position needs filling because your team's visible passion and *espirit des corps* attracts like-minded individuals. Your organization's culture of excellence takes the time necessary and uses innovative techniques to thoroughly learn about each individual candidate's true past performance.

Think about what that looks like, and write down a description of what you see. Who is in the room? What are they excited about in the new candidates?

Now think about what steps you need to take to get there – who needs to give their buy-in? How will you get your team enthusiastic about the process? What resources do you need to gather to make this happen?

The time and effort you put into hiring gives back in many ways beyond just the great people you bring onto the team. If you take the time to think about this and put your thoughts on paper, you will be on the way to having a world-class hiring process that attracts Relentless Innovators – your next step to *Building a Culture to Win.*

"The importance of chemistry and trust. High-performance teams look at much more than résumés and credentials in their personnel selection process."

U.S. Navy Photo Taken By MC3 Andrew Johnson

Chapter 3:

Fostering Chemistry, Core Values, and Trust

Building a Better Team

E arly July 2002: The Day of Reckoning for the 15 Blue Angel candidates who made it to the final round of interviews for the 2003 team. As I sat at my desk in the hangar that housed the Blue Angels' F/A-18 Hornets, I prepared for the hardest part of being the Boss – turning down 10 amazing candidates.

Only five would survive.

After the interviews ended just one week before, the finalists had each flown to their home base and were to call me at a prescheduled time to find out if they made it.

Our team had been up almost all night the night before, deliberating. The decision was hard because our options were all so good. To be among the finalists is an honor in itself, as they represent the elite pilots, maintenance and supply officers, and flight surgeons from the Navy and Marine Corps. Some of them had been vying for the team for several years, and to be selected would have been the culmination of a lifelong dream.

So as I prepared for the phone calls to come, I remember thinking what a privilege it is to be able to handpick our team from such a talented pool. I was essentially living every CEO's dream – we were selecting the most technically proficient Relentless Innovators, who also had the person-alities, values and character that would make it fun and rewarding to tackle the incredible challenges we would face over the next year.

We were going to succeed with style and have fun doing it.

Chemistry: Creating a "Family"

The deliberations during the selection process for both TOPGUN and the Blue Angels will always remain confi-dential. However, the results of the selection process are clear – we build an elite team whose members enjoy being together, even under the most stressful circumstances.

Elite teams require extensive time to focus on becoming the best, both technically and culturally. This is true across the board from sports teams to industry. It certainly is true at the Blue Angels and TOPGUN. You need people who can create and maintain a positive reinforcing chemistry within the team. They get excited about tackling tough challenges together.

The Blue Angels Diamond and Solo pilots are an extreme example. The six pilots spend almost every available hour of every day together from December through March. This is to just prepare for the show season.

They extensively pre-brief, fly and thoroughly debrief for two-to-three practices every day. Then, during the show season – March through mid-November – this grueling pace increases to add travel and air show performances to the continuous practice and training. Public commitments are constant and the team is always "on stage" regardless of where it is.

Additionally, the six pilots also require rigorous physical training every day so they can pull up to 7.5 Gs without the protection of a G-suit. A G-suit wraps around and squeezes the pilot's legs and lower abdomen to prevent the pilot from blacking out under high G-load. Unfortunately, the G-suit also interferes with the precise control movements necessary to fly very tight formations—so the Blue Angels do not use them.

The six pilots spend almost every waking hour with each other in this very intense environment. The process of mastering every element of the show can be stressful as new maneuvers are introduced every week, and the team begins to fly closer each day. The team has developed a culture of excellence that selects individuals who thrive in this kind of fast-paced environment.

Stress, doubt, and frustration can never be allowed to creep into this environment. The effects are corrosive to the team. That is why elite teams always look like they are enjoying what they do, no matter where they are on the scale of mastery that particular day. Their culture of excellence promotes the positive and immediately crushes any hint of negativity.

To be clear, they are always highly critical of their performance. The extensive and intense flight debriefs that we will discuss in a later chapter are very frank. The team needs individuals who can both dish out and take constructive criticism every day as they seek to relentlessly improve.

World-class teams do not waste energy on being negative. They select individuals who, in addition to being Relentless Innovators, have positive and constructive attitudes. They help create positive chemistry and personal dynamics within the team — and it shows!

When I was an air-wing commander and I had seven squadrons reporting to me on the ship, I could always judge how each squadron was doing by sensing the atmosphere in the ready-room. The performance metrics always confirmed my observations.

The ready-room on an aircraft carrier is a place where naval aviators build their bonds. It is where you sit for pre and post-mission briefings and debriefings. You and your fellow aviators are keyed up and focused. Yet, we still leave room for both levity and frank discussions.

The best squadrons always had a great ready-room atmosphere. The aircrew liked being there and positive energy was always at a high level. Not only were they good at their professional duty, they were excited to be there doing it. These organizations were full of winners.

The Blue Angels and TOPGUN also had ready-rooms. The Blues set one up at every air show site in a borrowed hangar space, conference room, or hotel. It is where they conduct very serious air show briefings and debriefings. The culture of excellence demands and selects team players that promote this positive professional approach, no matter where the room is located.

Selecting the Next Generation

The fact is, not every Relentless Innovator can work well with others. Finding the individuals who not only have the skills, but who have what it takes to enhance the chemistry of the team, embrace the culture, and make the group story their story is essential to fostering and maintaining a culture of excellence. Anything less weakens an organization.

I have learned keys to picking winning teams from selecting people for the Blue Angels, TOPGUN, and four-star generals' staffs, as well as industry. The same principles – the importance of chemistry and matching core values as the tiebreakers between candidates – apply to any organization.

Howard Schultz, CEO of Starbucks, said it best:

> "Great companies are not based on great strategies. Great companies that are enduring and sustainable are based on great people who have like-minded values and are all pointed in the right direction[1]."

I have found no metric you can measure to reliably score these intangibles. Therefore, it comes down to developing a process that allows you to get a clear sense about someone. The Blue Angels, again, has a great example of this process in action.

Core Values: "Glad To Be Here"

When I was first introduced to the Blue Angels, before I became a member myself, I had the opportunity to fly in the back of a two-seat F/A-18 during a practice demonstration. Not only was I amazed at the level of professionalism of everyone on the team, but I was also totally impressed with their attitudes.

"Glad to be here." That's a saying all the Blues say at the beginning and ending of every brief and every flight. Why? Because when the daily grind gets difficult and challenging, they could easily forget what a privilege it is to fly for the Blues. The phrase "Glad to be here" reminds

---

1   (From University of Denver, Daniels College of Business *2011-2012 Progress Report*)

team members that it is a privilege to be part of such a world-class team.

It is a combination of "thanks," "good day," and "best wishes," but it goes even further. Each time the team says, "Glad to be here," they reaffirm their commitment to the shared core values of the team. Even though the job gets tough, the team understands that their hard work is all for the common good.

A person's character is a reflection of their core values. While difficult to perfectly define, it is important to make clear a basic framework of what is expected and put it in writing.

Both TOPGUN and the Blue Angels have personal and professional codes of conduct. The team members are always expected to self-critique and acknowledge publicly to the team any violation. Sincerely embracing the team's core values and standards shows character, especially when you are expected to uphold them when no one else is around.

For example, the Blues have a dress code and grooming standards that apply whether you are in public or on your own personal time. Team members would often acknowledge violations, no matter how minor, during our team meetings. Knowing that your teammates are as serious as you are at upholding the standards, strengthens passion, promotes free will and helps focus the team on what is truly important – facing the challenge of the job.

Upholding Your Contract

The Blue Angels operate in one of the most unforgiving environments, where precision is a must. The margins are quite literally very small. As a result, we had unwritten flying contracts that were absolute. Everyone had to uphold them or death would result.

My contract as the Boss leading the team was, "I will never fly the formation into the ground." The wingman's contracts were, "We will never hit the Boss or each other." Pretty simple, right? Well, because of the speeds, altitudes, and close proximity to each other, honoring these contracts requires all of your skill and attention. Throughout winter training and the show season, the team members develop more and more trust in each other and the team gets tighter and flies better.

Eventually, we are ready for the Double Farvel.

The Double Farvel is a complex, high-precision formation during which half the Diamond is flying upside down. Trust is necessary at every phase of this maneuver. First the Boss has to line the formation up at just the right distance to the right of the air show center-point, and at just the right airspeed and altitude. Then the Boss and the #4 pilot must flip their jets upside down while in tight formation, without hitting the wingmen. They must then make smooth control movements – the opposite direction than they normally do

– to make corrections as the Diamond flies in front of the crowd.

The maneuver becomes even more complicated in towns with radio and cell towers that are right on the show line and that must be threaded like a needle—while upside down.

"Success in the Double Farvel is achieved through trust from the wrench turner, to your crew chief and ultimately your fellow pilots!"
Photo by Bernard Zee©

Obviously, the maneuver requires a great deal of trust, not only among all team members – wingmen and Boss – but also with the maintenance crew. Aircraft have to be 100 percent correct, and crew chiefs need to prepare and strap the pilots into the seat perfectly so they do not fall out while upside down and lose control of the jet. The right wingman has the critical job of punching a stopwatch at roll in and calling for the Boss to finish the maneuver before the inverted fuel tanks run dry.

If any of these elements are missing, disaster can happen.

Pilots, just like your team, can only pull a Double Farvel – pushing themselves to their limits – when they have complete trust in themselves, their teammates, and their equipment.

Trust: The Team Comes First

Trust extends to assuming that everyone will put the team first – even when their own life is on the line. When selecting someone for an elite team, I want to know they are sincere about putting the team first.

The Blue Angels do everything in their power to fly the safest air show in the world. There are times when one must self-sacrifice to ensure the team's overall safety. The Diamond takeoff is a great example.

During this maneuver, all four F/A-18s accelerate down the runway together in close formation. In the event one of the Boss's two engines fails, requiring him to abort his takeoff, he cannot apply the brakes and throttle back the other engine until the other three wingman behind him have safely slowed their aircraft to avoid collision.

This means that at some point the Boss may have to run off

the end of the runway to ensure the safety of his team.

High-performance teams that share chemistry and core values – as well as outstanding skills and expertise – have members that trust each other. In the best teams, business development, engineering, finance, and research all trust each other to do their jobs, do them well, and do them on time. They usually follow the example set by their sector presidents and vice presidents. The best of them will "run off the end of the runway" for their team in supporting their efforts. Otherwise, the team is weakened.

When team members trust each other they function in a seamless fashion that maximizes the value of each individual and supercharges the organization as a whole.

Making the Call

Back in that hangar in 2002 on the verge of taking the phone calls from excited Navy and Marine Corps airmen and women, I thought to myself what an awesome process and culture we inherited from previous teams dating back to 1946.

The team has an aggressive, thorough and meticulous hiring culture. It was fun and professionally rewarding. New friends were made and a lot was learned – both ways – in the process. Every relevant piece of information gathered over a period of months, and in some cases years, was used.

We went well beyond mere skill evaluation. We understood the applicants' core values, aspirations and goals. We knew if they truly were Relentless Innovators, and we knew we could trust them to put the team's priorities first. The new selectees would need all of that to be successful over their next few years on the team.

The applicants each called in at their appropriate time slots. Like other parts of the Blue Angels selection process, the particulars of the phone calls will always remain confidential. But each time, I was reassured that we had a great process. All the non-selects, although disappointed, remarked how much they enjoyed getting to know the team.

You know you have perpetuated a great culture, when the new hire's response to hearing the great news of their selection is, "Glad to be here, Boss!"

Points to Remember

1. It is critical for harmonizing The Performance Triad that each member is a Relentless Innovator with common core values, which leads to good chemistry and ultimately to complete trust.

2. Team members must have good chemistry so that you can create a close-knit group that can candidly critique performances and work to improve based on feedback.

3. World-class teams that share the same core values

will truly be "Glad to be here," even when times are tough because they know the job will not be easy, but it will be rewarding.

4. Team members cannot be expected to perform at their best unless they have complete trust in all team members, from support crew all the way up to the Boss.

Chair Flying Exercise

Visualize yourself in your office on a very challenging day. Your largest client, customer, or donor has just called to say that they have had a technical complication that will delay their check to your company, division, or organization. Your largest vendor is expecting your check today or they will not ship the item or perform the service on time for you to deliver to your own clients or customers.

Are you feeling stressed? Are you pacing? Who are you contacting in your company, division, or your organization to ensure that things run as smoothly as possible? What members of your team are working together to solve the problem? What members are likely refusing to work together? How do you see the final outcome of the situation?

Now imagine yourself in the same situation of a late customer and a time-sensitive vendor, but this time you are relaxing in a comfortable chair in your office. You are thinking about your next meeting that will move the company, division, or organization forward. You are not distracted by a large financial glitch. Your team will handle it and keep you informed.

In this more relaxed scenario, who in your company, division or organization is responsible for making sure that no single late receivable or urgent payable – no matter how large – will affect your team's ability to make sure your business flows properly? What do you need to do to make sure this happens? Do you need to work on trust among members? Do you need to re-evaluate the core values you want in your team? What improvements need to happen to ensure that your team is as effective and efficient as it can be – to be world-class?

"World-class organizations have cultures that relentlessly pursue great communication and team alignment from before takeoff to after landing. The Boss starts the show sequence with his command, Smoke On."

U.S. Navy Photo Taken By MC2 Rachel McMarr

Chapter 4:
Aligning the Team

All Together Now – "Up We Go . . ."

It is November, and we're waiting to take off on our final show of the season in sunny Pensacola, FL. As Boss, I have the privilege of sitting in the #1 spot – smack dab in the middle of four shining blue and gold F/A-18 fighter jets at the end of the runway.

My team and I are lined up in fingertip formation, which looks like the fingertips of your right hand. The Boss (#1) is your middle finger. The right wingman (#2) is the ring finger. The left wingman (#3) is the index finger, and the slot pilot (#4) is the pinky finger.

"The Blue Angels rolling down the runway in full afterburner leading into a take-off loop."

Photo By Bernard Zee ©

As Boss, my job is to lead the team through voice calls that serve as the drummer of a rock band, creating and keeping a tempo that we can all follow. This synchronicity will allow all three Diamond wingmen to fly extremely close as all four of us execute our stick-and-throttle movements together.

As I am given clearance to take off, I start my cadence: "We're cleared for takeoff, the winds are calm, check your parking brake off, check your trim set. Maneuver is Diamond Burner Loop with a right turn out." The team acknowledges my commands. I then command the engine run up, "Let's run 'em up."

I look over to my right and left to receive a visual thumbs-up from each of my wingmen. "Smoke on... off brakes now... burners ready now," I say as we begin the show.

A huge cloud of air show smoke billows behind the formation, as the 36,000 pounds of thrust per aircraft has our body weight pushing us firmly against our seats. All four jets accelerate down the runway in very tight formation. Within a few seconds, we have reached 150 knots, as we begin to lift off.

I call out several command bursts "Gear," "A little drive," "Up we go...a little more *pulllll*." My team is in synch with my tempo, understanding that timing is everything. They know to keep pulling on the control stick until the last "L" in "pullll" is sounded. I sense the #4 jet move into the slot position behind me.

The Diamond is now performing a loop at three times the pull of gravity and is shooting through thousands of feet in altitude in a matter of seconds. The goal is to complete the loop maneuver almost where it started with a safety buffer of a couple hundred feet, and to do it in a smooth manner so that the wingmen can maintain the very tight formation throughout.

We rely on the timing, tempo and the "muscle memory" the team has developed over hundreds of practices to safely complete the maneuver without hitting each other or the ground.

The importance of critical alignment is clear when the Blue Angels maintain such a tight formation – wing tips and canopy to wing-tip distances are mere inches apart. The Boss never moves his airplane without making a call in a predictable manner.

As in business, the Boss's cadence must be steady, synchronizing his team's stick-and-throttle movements precisely so we can reach our goal without crashing.

In the Blues, if the Boss or a team member rushes a maneuver or changes the cadence of communication and action, the formation becomes misaligned and people can run into each other, causing serious issues. Everything must be in synch if you are going to have a high-performing, world-class organization – from the Chief to the entry-level team member.

World-Class Teams Work on Alignment from Day One

One of the most exciting and inspirational days for me as a Blue Angel was the very first day of winter training with the new team. It did not involve any flying.

The day was dedicated to getting the entire team aligned and reviewing the basics. Everyone was in attendance from the Boss down to the administrators and maintenance crew. The whole Blue Angels organization gathers and reviews command history, core values and mission. The annual goals developed by various dedicated teams were also discussed. We got buy-in at every level through participation.

Additionally, and most importantly, the Blue Angels code of conduct was reviewed. This included the very basics of how as Blue Angels we were expected dress, appear, and interact in public. By the end of the day, everyone was reminded of what it meant to be a Blue Angel.

This happened every single year, without exception. We never took it for granted that everyone was in synch. We made getting everyone in synch part of our daily lives.

Coach Wooden on Alignment and Focus

For anyone who thinks that this attention to detail and planning is a military phenomenon, consider UCLA Varsity Basketball Coach John Wooden. In the early 1960s to mid-1970s, Coach Wooden led his teams to numerous national championships.

When Coach Wooden started a season, he welcomed all the players, and said, "Let's get down to business." He then gave the team his words of wisdom, but they were not the words the players had expected. He told his team about the rules he expected them to follow as UCLA basketball players: Keep your fingernails trimmed, your hair short, and your jerseys tucked into your trunks.

At first, the players thought the coach must be joking. When they realized he was serious, they were shocked. Why was Coach Wooden making such a big deal out of such little details?

Far from being insignificant, these details were vital to the performance of the team. Short fingernails, short hair, and properly worn jerseys translate into higher overall performance – in other words, if you focus on doing the little things right, that will translate into greatness in the big picture.

When you strive for excellence while doing the small things – never, ever allowing sloppiness to creep in – that precise, meticulous dynamic becomes part of your team's overall method, both in practice and in execution.

Before the NCAA tournament finals in Louisville in 1967, the team gathered together for Coach Wooden's pregame talk. He went to the chalkboard, and the team expected him to diagram a new tactic or play he wanted them to try.

Instead, he illustrated where he wanted the players to stand while the national anthem was being played. Then he told them how he expected them to behave after the game, in light of the bad behavior of another team the day before.

He never said a word about the specifics of the upcoming game or UCLA's opponent that day. He clearly figured he had already taught the players what they needed to know, which had started that first day when he told them he expected short fingernails, short hair, and tucked-in jerseys. He had begun with the basics.

Coach Wooden understood the importance of team alignment. He was also a master at balancing passion and free will with the right amount of focus to win. They did win that day – 79 to 64 over Dayton – and became national champions.

Aligning the "Newbies" into the Team

The Blue Angels call new teammates, "newbies." By tradition, an individual is considered a newbie for their first eight months on the team. During that time, they immerse themselves in the team's legacy and its culture of excellence. At the end, they are expected to have made the organization's story their own—they are now truly part of the team.

It is an inspirational transformation to becoming a Blue Angel. It is not about breaking anyone – it is about individuals bringing their personal capabilities and passion into alignment with those of the others on the team.

Once newbies have earned the trust of the rest of the team they become, in everyone's mind, full team and family members.

"Cultures of excellence have indoctrination processes that instill a sense of family and ownership in the organization – after months of hard work, this individual is ceremoniously being welcomed into the family and is now part of its legacy."

Photo by Trent Kalp©

Maximizing Alignment and Chemistry Through Careful Placement of the Relentless Innovators

Recruiting excellent candidates is obviously important to the Blue Angels, as is the newbie process. The team rapidly integrates new recruits and makes them family.

Cultures of excellence also maximize team alignment by considering continuity and chemistry when placing new hires.

First, continuity. The Blue Angels have very specialized skill sets that are required for their air show demonstrations. These skills are unique and found nowhere else in the Navy. Therefore, to maintain team alignment, it is critical to have a continuity plan whereby the experience and nuances of each position in the formation are directly passed from one generation to the next.

In the Blue Angels, the Boss position turns over every two years. Everybody else in the Diamond Formation has some kind of movement or training responsibility shift in the process, which helps maintain continuity. For example, during my first year as Boss, the left wingman, #3, was also on his first year on the team. We learned the maneuvers from the right wingman, #2, and the slot pilot, #4, who were seasoned second-year Blue Angels.

Then, during my second year as Boss, the previous #3 rotated to become the new #4 and we trained a new #2 and #3. That continuity dynamic continues from year-to-year and it works great for the Blue Angels.

In business, the best performing organization considers continuity when making personnel changes as a way to maximize alignment. Not only are you passing on training for each position, but you are also spreading a fuller understanding of the company and how each department works.

Chemistry is next. World-class teams consider chemistry for maintaining alignment. For example, the Blue Angels Solo pilots work closely with each other every day, since the Lead Solo teaches the Opposing Solo for continuity. The right chemistry between the two is critical because without it, the Lead's constant critiques could cause strain in the relationship and lead to deteriorating performance.

Great chemistry promotes great communication and elevates everyone's spirit. Next time you see what you think is a great team, observe how the team members interact with each other, and how much fun they look like they are having.

I have seen teams maintain high morale and positive energy through some of the most challenging conditions, including combat, because they have great chemistry and, thus, great alignment.

World-Class Teams have Cultures that Focus on Enhancing Alignment Every Day through Great Communication

The best organizations work hard and inspire everyone by maintaining great communications both up and down the chain of command, as well as laterally. This holistic communication is usually accomplished through a communication battle rhythm that has become part of those organizations' cultures.

Two organizations with the widest ranging global operations in the military, for which I had the pleasure of working, were the Joint Chiefs of Staff and North American Aerospace Defense Command/U.S. Northern Command (NORAD/U.S. NORTHCOM).

Both of these organizations had to maintain alignment with the other four-star regional and functional combatant commands, as well as with our international partners. They also had to maintain alignment with the President of the United States and other governmental departments such as the State Department.

Both organizations had very effective battle rhythms, which provide a way for everyone on a team to connect with one another and which also facilitate alignment.

Battle rhythm is the timing and tempo of information flow. It synchronizes critical meetings so decision-makers get the important information they need at the right time.

In my advisor capacity in business, I can tell almost immediately whether there is alignment at the top and throughout the organization.

For example a vice president can unwittingly undermine the direction set by the president if he or she is not showing sufficient commitment or is perhaps draining off focus on a subsidiary effort. The president can contribute to this by releasing corporate data erratically or having meetings without proper notice so staff can prepare.

Working out-of-step always leads to poor performance because it creates confusion and distraction.

By contrast, cultures of excellence develop ways of working through these types of differences so that there is a high level of coordination and support between and among functions in the organization.

Battle rhythm shows in the tactical and day-to-day operations. However, the rhythm should extend for longer periods for strategic reasons.

For example, to achieve overall alignment, you need a way to get everyone together to talk about big-picture issues such as the organization's mission and vision. This get-together is usually a big event that happens maybe once a year. Ideally, you then have daily, weekly, and monthly battle rhythm activities you conduct to strengthen alignment throughout the organization.

In the Joint Chiefs, NORAD, and NORTHCOM, department heads would take information back and distribute to their departments as needed. Town-hall-style meetings were used as well, but mainly for big announcements, because they could not serve as the sole method of communication for a whole organization.

One interesting thing about battle rhythm for the Joint Chiefs, NORAD and NORTHCOM: It was a consistent drum beat whether things were going smoothly or they were in crisis mode. The battle rhythm pretty much worked the same way regardless of what was going on because it was established.

Even when additional meetings with external organizations like FEMA and the Department of Homeland Security were layered in on top of what these world-class organizations already had in place, their battle rhythm did not change. The Joint Chiefs, NORAD, and NORTHCOM could handle any contingency – and easily make it march to their battle rhythms.

World-Class Teams Take Whatever Time is Needed to Ensure Alignment

A TOPGUN staff instructor's meeting is known as a *Stafex*. They are legendary in the Navy for their length and thoroughness. They constitute a critical element in ensuring alignment throughout TOPGUN and the rest of the Naval Aviation community. They are legendary because they achieve alignment by a process I call the *"Brute Force Method."*

When I was a TOPGUN instructor, I found myself with my fellow instructors working late at night. We all had long ago called home to tell families that we were not going to make it home for dinner.

Since TOPGUN instructors are responsible for standard-izing the fighter tactics that the fleet uses in combat, all of us were constantly searching for the best tactic against the threats our peers were facing in overseas combat.

When we had particular issues to decide, the rule was that we were not going home until we had finished. Often, that meant staying very late at night, with heated discussions and differences of opinion. Our focus helped us harness our free will and our passion to work through the tough issues.

For communication to work well, people must feel free to honestly talk about differences of opinion. The TOPGUN method is called *Brute Force* because it is hard and because it continues until you come to an agreement.

After the decision was accepted, it became the naval standard, or STAN. TOPGUN instructors were expected to espouse it at all times. This ensured that our students and the Navy were always aligned as well—no one ever saw a difference of opinion from a TOPGUN instructor, and therefore everyone would follow that same tactic.

In cultures of excellence, it's vital that people on all levels of the chain of command be able to articulate and discuss their differences, using their free will. Then, with the decision made by the team and leadership, even if it is against what you think is best, support it and move on... or get out.

You Have Alignment When Everyone on the Team Can Be a Credible Spokesman

Can everyone in your organization articulate your mission and your vision as well as you can? I've learned that everyone in a world-class organization is – and should be – a company spokesperson.

In the case of the Blues, I was always very comfortable with media attention because each person on the team, from the Boss to the technician turning wrenches, could articulately speak to any reporter about the mission of the Blues.

In the air and on the ground, the Blue Angels are always aligned.

I am reminded of an Airframes Machinist's Mate Second Class. His nickname was "Cruiser." He gave some of the most memorable media interviews I can remember. He was a great example of the high quality individuals we had on the team. He was also a great example of how well we were aligned as an organization.

I recall being in a hotel room at a show site, reviewing my maneuvers for the air show. At the same time, I was catching news clips from media footage about the show. Cruiser happened to get picked at random to do an interview by a local news channel.

As I watched the clip, I knew I would be happy with his performance because everyone on the team knew how to handle themselves with the media. Since it was just after 9-11, though, and we had a vital role in giving our country confidence in our military, I watched intently to make sure he struck just the right note.

Cruiser was spectacular. At the time of the interview, he had just finished a repair on a jet, but he spoke magnificently and looked great. His demeanor was perfect for the situation: confident, direct, articulate, and reverent.

He was able to describe the mission of the Blue Angels and how it related to national security. He also related the vision and goals of what we were doing at the Blue Angels, and how they were representative of the men and women who were deployed overseas. He struck a patriotic tone that instilled confidence, calmness, and an assurance to all those watching – including me!

All in all, that interview was one of the best I've ever seen from anyone at any level. It was genuine; it came from the heart. Cruiser believed in our mission, and it came across that way. He was passionate and you could tell it was his passion and free will doing the talking – not just something he had been told to say.

I am convinced that this one video clip has recruited thousands more young men and women just like him and has given the American public a glimpse into the outstanding volunteers who protect our country every day. You couldn't help but be proud.

Even though I was the Boss and by position the head team spokesperson, realistically, we had an entire organization of individuals just like Cruiser who were far more effective in telling our story than I could ever be by myself.

Points to Remember

1. World-class teams have cultures that constantly work to align the organization down to the smallest detail.

2. The alignment of goals, timing and tempo must be set prior to starting any new business line, project, or yearly strategy session.

3. Battle rhythm establishes communication expectations between players to ensure there is alignment in the daily routine, organizational processes and even messaging.

Chair Flying Exercise

Imagine your company or organization being awarded the largest project in its history. You will need to bring in a few new employees to work alongside those who have been with you for years. The deadline for delivery is tight. If you are going to make this project work, every step of the process, every member of the team must work in perfect alignment. If the process breaks down, the delivery will not be made and you will be out millions of dollars.

What are some of the issues that your team would face if this project happened today? Would everyone be ready to go? Would the leadership team be able to communicate a clear vision and a clear plan to the whole team? Does every person on your team have someone who can cover for them if they become ill or fall behind? Who are your weak links? Is it the newbies?

Think about what processes you need to create in your company to fulfill that big order. What training do you need to provide? Who are your weakest links? Who are your Relentless Innovators who will lead your team and work with you to improve the process along the way? If you do not have anyone you trust to step up and take the lead in any scenario, what can you do to develop this in your current team?

Visualize how you would like the process to run, and then think about what you need to put in place to make the reality match the ideas forming in your head.

*"Teams with cultures built around The Performance Triad,
launch into the most difficult "dark" environments with complete
confidence that they will win!"*

U.S. Navy Photo Taken By MC3 Bryan Reckard

Section 2:

Time to Execute -

Taking the CATSHOT, Flying the Mission and Staying Focused until the End

The Flight Deck of a U.S. aircraft carrier is a noisy, dynamic yet peaceful place.

As I sit strapped into the cockpit, I am so focused I can barely hear a thing, but I can see team members moving around the deck, checking things out, talking on their intercommunication systems and signaling each other as the engines of our jets roar.

I know that the mission has been planned; the aircraft has been fueled, armed, and completely checked out; and the pilot is strapped in and ready to go. Now, the catapult will be pulled back like a rubber band with a multi-million-dollar rock poised in it.

My years of training and experience with my team make me confident that everyone has done their job well. I trust them. Otherwise, I would not be here. One wrong move and I would be catapulted into the sea, never to be seen again.

The next move is to go to full power. I trust that the special holdback mechanism has been installed between the flight deck and my aircraft. I take my feet off the brakes, check my instruments and wipe out (move) all of the control surfaces. When I am ready for flight, I salute the Catapult Officer. On deck, the Final Checkers are observing the exterior of the aircraft and, when satisfied, will give a thumb's up to the Catapult Officer.

Everyone is in alignment.

Then and only then, the Cat Officer makes his absolute final check and gives the signal to launch to the catapult operator – who fires the catapult, taking me from a dead stop to 150 Knots almost instantly.

The acceleration is like nothing else on Earth. It slams your whole body into the back of the ejection seat. It is constant, it never fades until . . . BAM! . . . the catapult slams into its breaking mechanism at the end of its track and you are set free. You are flying.

That is a CATSHOT!

Until this moment, everything was just preparation. Now, we are on the move.

"*Capable of more than just a spectacular takeoff performance, the all U.S. Marine Fat Albert team, "The Bert Boys" are an example of the behind-the-scenes culture of excellence needed to keep a world-class organization consistently operating at peak capacity.*"

U.S. Navy Photo

Chapter 5:
Inspire, Plan, and "Move Out"

Looking Into the Belly of the Beast

Packing up six pilots, 50 support personnel, and seven precision aircraft is not as easy as it sounds.

Fat Albert, the self-contained C-130 Transport Aircraft, is packed with precision. The Blue Angels only have one such aircraft, and it must hold all of their spare parts, tools, support personnel and all of their gear. A team of travel experts must move everyone and everything to weekly practices and air shows. From mid-March until November, the team travels to over 30 sites around the United States for air shows. The travel team makes sure cars, hotel rooms, and meals are all laid out for us in each town and in exacting fashion.

Even though the Blues travel with one extra airplane and all the essential extra parts, they do not have an extra pilot. Therefore, it is imperative that the pilots are healthy, on-time and properly equipped.

While the Blue Angels do not head into battle, they are on a mission – touring the nation and performing at air shows for 300 days a year as ambassadors of goodwill. As such, we had to be spot-on perfect for every show. The battle rhythm of perfection in our performances had to be sustained between shows as we moved and maintained aircraft, obtained supplies, and saw to the health and personal needs of our team.

Our moves demanded a lot of discipline, family and personal sacrifice, and planning. We all had roles to play and a schedule to keep. And we worked hard to plan ahead. Our planning was made more effective and easier because everyone was onboard. We were aligned and synchronized. All members of the crew understood the mission, and were committed to its success.

Any organization can achieve the same level of success on their mission – whether it is launching a new product, revamping a retail store, or implementing a new corporate strategy. The entire team needs to be onboard and motivated to reach the same goal together. Leadership needs to recognize the rhythm and pace that the mission will demand. An exciting kick-off event is not enough. The entire performance must be in-synch from beginning to end.

Any kind of change—whether it is making changes to an

air show routine or reengineering a corporation—takes buy-in from all levels of the organization.

At TOPGUN, we got buy-in for strategic efforts and for other organizational change through our Stafex process, namely *"The Brute Force Alignment Method."* In Stafex, we deliberated until we reached STAN, or standardization. Sometimes the discussions would last until late in the night. That was fine, because we took all the time we needed to get buy-in from the whole team.

The Blue Angels has a similar tactic whereby everyone gets together and discusses strategy. All team members review the mission and get input from people throughout the command. They take all the information that has come from everyone and compile it into a master strategy, which the team members approve.

When working in large organizations where buy-in from entire staffs may seem impractical, leaders can identify their own elite team, such as their direct reports, with whom they can create STAN. In turn, those direct reports should encourage and gather feedback from their staffs, so that everyone has an opportunity to have their voices heard, up and down the chain of command. This practice can take a lot of time, but will pay off in the end.

For elite teams, each person in an organization must feel like his or her voice is being heard to ensure that they all have complete confidence in the plan, especially at the moment difficulties arise in the execution of the plan. It is difficult times that pose challenges to a team's alignment and inspiration on all levels.

This intense process is a great example of The Performance Triad – passion, free will, and focus – in action. It served us well under the most trying circumstances anyone could imagine.

Dedicated to Freedom: Inspirational Strategic Planning

It was November in my second year as Boss of the Blue Angels, and in Blue Angels tradition, we were in the process of developing our strategic plan. The year was 2001; the plan was to be for 2002.

"Who would have imagined this would be the last flyby of the Twin Towers? Roaring back after 9-11, the country stayed true to the Founding Father's vision of a nation built on a culture of excellence!"

U.S. Navy Photo

To the public, the Blues represent all of the men and women of the Armed Forces, though they are technically Navy and Marine airmen and women. So a vital part of the coming year's strategic plan would be for us to assure the American public that their military was there for them and to show the public our professionalism.

In June 2001, we had done low altitude flying over New York City during which we took panoramic images for a lithograph. We had visions of presenting an amazing shot of the skyline to Mayor Giuliani and the people of New York City.

Due to weather conditions, however, the photos turned out less than ideal. A haze that hung over the Northeast U.S. that day dulled the photo. We were disappointed that we would not be able to use them.

Three months later, the 9-11 attacks occurred and those snapshots took on a poignancy that no one could ever have foreseen. With the photos, we created a lithograph – our aircraft and the pre-attack New York Skyline – called, "Dedicated to Freedom."

The outpouring of support from everyone who saw the lithograph was amazing. They told us it was a truly inspiring image. "Dedicated to Freedom" then became our theme for the coming year's strategic plan. This theme helped us focus our plan on that inspiration.

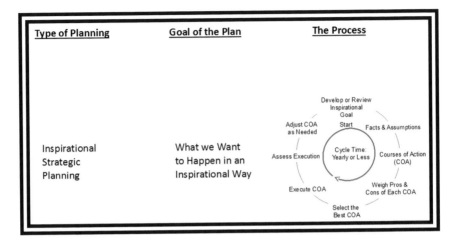

Type of Planning	Goal of the Plan	The Process
Inspirational Strategic Planning	What we Want to Happen in an Inspirational Way	

Inspirational strategic planning is a concept that the Blue Angels embraced before 9-11, but it took on a whole new dimension after 9-11. It is a concept that all world-class organizations have in their culture. The Blue Angels of 2001 reflected the national sentiment and found itself with inspiration of epic proportions that year.

You and your organization can easily find your own inspiration, whether it is launching a breakthrough new product, revolutionizing a process that has been unchanged for years, or leading your team to reach aggressive new revenue goals that will allow you to upgrade your facilities.

The basic concept of inspirational strategic planning is that you must find a new goal that inspires your team to work together to reach it. The plan needs to mean something to everyone in the organization.

To be successful, you must clearly communicate the plan to the team, and challenge them to consider everything that must change—down to the tiniest detail. It is up to your leadership to manage the execution of the plan—to motivate people and set a battle rhythm—and set the course of action that embraces The Performance Triad of your team members.

Our strategic plan for "Dedicated to Freedom" included the goal to tighten up our shows, which had grown to be about 45 minutes long.

In light of everything we were already doing right, we still wanted to take things to the next level and make our shows even more exciting. To figure out how to do this, my flight crew and I talked to the ground crew, former Blue Angels, and some of our biggest fans.

As a result of these talks, we realized that to give the show more excitement, we needed to get rid of the long stretches between the sequential maneuvers of the show.

Our challenge was to do the same number of maneuvers, but in less time.

We examined the periods during which we were waiting for planes to get set up and do passes to see how we could get back in front of the crowd in the shortest amount of time. We also had to consider ways to do this smoothly so the wingman could maintain formation while pulling excessive G-forces.

Because the Blue Angels alternate on the show line between the Diamond maneuvers and the Solos maneuvers, I had to work hard with the lead Solo pilot, and opposing Solo pilot. We were all vested in the concept of looking as precise as possible while moving the show along faster and making it more thrilling for the audience. This passion permeated throughout the whole organization, from pilots to support personnel.

With our goal of speeding up the demo in our sites throughout the season, we methodically became more precise. As a result, the shows became tighter and faster. Working together throughout the year, we were able to chop 10 minutes off our shows – a great achievement. It was an achievement that required the entire team be fully engaged, and fully inspired, to reach the goal together.

Stoke Enthusiasm Through Internal Feedback

"Cultures of excellence value feedback from all levels – like my crew chief."
Photo by Toru EBISAWA©

Our team faced a lot of roadblocks along the journey to our goal. We found a lot of great ideas on how to overcome those roadblocks from all people in all areas of our operation. Some of the most constructive feedback we received on how to improve the show came from our support personnel, not just the demonstration pilots.

My two ground crew chiefs would give blunt assessment after every practice or show. I trusted and used their feedback to continually fine-tune our plan. The side benefit to this process was that they knew I valued their input because I incorporated many of their suggestions.

Over time, when people know their feedback is both necessary and desired for the betterment of the whole team, enthusiasm is amped up and their participation leads to fervent support and passionate execution of the team's plan.

After we shortened the show to a much more dynamic 35 minutes, we still faced the challenge of getting the word out about our show and gaining visibility.

As popular as the Blue Angels are, many Americans still had never been to an air show and had never seen us perform. Just as with speeding up our shows, team enthusiasm for our media-related goals permeated the entire organization.

Our Public Affairs officer was aggressive. He went way outside the box of conventional media coverage to work with the Discovery Channel to get a documentary crew to follow the team around for a year. It was a real break-through, a chance to increase awareness of our perfor-mances and us, and also a chance to share some aspects of our culture.

Setting in motion a significant increase in media exposure not only provided a wonderful wrap-up to our "Dedicated to Freedom" year, but it also set the stage for a series of subsequent media engagements and documentary re-runs that spanned several more years and continued to help with the mission of the Blues.

Blues in Business – Inspiration 101

The greatest achievements of mankind were fueled by visions, goals that sparked the passion in individuals to come together as teams and make things happen. When President John F. Kennedy set the challenge to the United States of going to the moon, he spoke these inspiring words:

"We choose to go to the moon in this decade ... because that goal will serve to organize and measure the best of our energies and skills, because that challenge is one that we are willing to accept, one we are unwilling to postpone, and one which we intend to win."

During my growing-up years, everyone was focused on the Space Race. I will never forget when Neil Armstrong set foot on the moon for the first time. It felt like the whole nation had pulled together to make John F. Kennedy's vision a reality.

Just as revolutionary were people like Bill Gates who had a vision of putting a computer on every desk, or the 1980 United States hockey team that focused on winning an Olympic gold medal for its country. The Founding Fathers also had an inspirational strategic plan for the United States: Leverage the promise of individual liberty as key to a great and thriving nation.

The keys to having a good plan with a vision are: (1) Make it simple, (2) Make it easy to understand, and (3) Make it easy to remember at every level. In short, there must be something in it for everyone.

Passion, focus, and free will are the starting points. When ground troops are out in the field, away from headquarters, they must understand their missions. Generals can't be everywhere.

Instead, generals must communicate the strategic plan and a passion for success to the troops in an understandable way and inspire them to carry it out with their free will; so they can focus on their mission and have the knowledge necessary to adapt to challenges that arise.

Getting the troops focused on the same page is absolutely essential. The Blue Angels get together to talk about strategic plans and goals for the year. Business leaders and professionals create their own corporate campaigns.

Ford Motor Company's famous slogan: "Quality is Job 1" was a great motivator for the company. When all team members are passionate about quality – the quality of their mission, the quality of their organization, and the quality of each team member's unique contributions – then they can all get onboard for planning, both for short-term goals and long-term goals. These plans get leveraged into inspirational strategies that keep on giving, to individuals and to the team as a whole.

Winning is not the only goal. The goal is one of developing a culture of excellence that will give you the very best chance of winning every time, and then executing the development of that culture and the plan to the best of the team's ability.

The best winning organizations focus on creating a culture that ingrains the elements of winning methodology into its DNA. An inspirational, strategic plan is a hallmark of a culture of excellence: planning to win, then inspiring the team to do whatever it takes to put forth its best efforts.

An inspirational plan, delivered to a team that has learned to promote and harness the power of passion, where team members trust each other, will adapt and continue to deliver, regardless of how the field of play changes. That agility needed to win is a product of each individual's mission understanding and the use of their free will to make smart, informed decisions that support the overall objective.

In other words, a culture of excellence promotes an attitude of independent, passionate thinking and executions tempered with the focus of complete and comprehensive mission understanding and buy-in.

Points to Remember

1. Inspirational strategic planning requires a big goal that motivates the entire team to pull together to make it work.

2. World-class organizations work hard to earn buy-in at all levels of an organization by asking for feedback from everyone and looking for ways to incorporate changes and input from all team members, not just those directly affected nor just those at the top of the organization.

3. A good plan with a vision is simple, easily under-standable, and easy to remember.

4. Cultures of excellence make the process of inspi-rational strategic planning part of their cultural makeup, its DNA.

Chair Flying Exercise

Think about the last three company-wide or organiza-tion-wide goals that you have implemented. Write a one-line description of each goal along the top of separate sheets of paper and lay them out in front of you. Add the approximate date of each from start to finish.

Now on each paper write the different names of the people in your organization/company if it is small, and the names of the departments, if it is a large organization/company. How was each of them involved in the goal? What was their contribution? If no involvement or contribution, then ask yourself why not. Did you ask them to be involved? Did you encourage them? Include them in meetings?

Visualize asking those who were not involved, or were barely involved, and imagine yourself approaching them and asking for their input. Do you see conflict? Complacency? Enthusiasm? What could you have done differently to engage them? Is there a process that you could implement for future projects that would include them, or encourage them to be more enthusiastic?

Imagine what it would look like to have everyone engaged – even your biggest naysayer or that one person who keeps to themselves. What can you do to make sure they are tapped for their input? What would it look like to have everyone engaged and onboard?

"Cultures of excellence make contingency planning formal and part of everyday operations."

U.S. Navy Photo

Chapter 6:
Contingency Planning for the Possibilities

W e are slicing through the desert sky, just north of El
Centro, California, in Blue Angels winter training.
The sun has peeked over the horizon a little more than an
hour ago. Our maneuvers have been in good synchronization for the first part of our practice demo.

As Boss, I make my radio calls to the guys, "Easing the pull,
rolling out the Diamond Dirty Loop." After a brief pause,
I add, "A little drive," to keep the nose of our aircraft from
ballooning up on rollout.

My wingmen acknowledge.

In a rhythmic cadence, I call, "Burner... ready... NOW."
BAM! The landing gears are down, the tailhooks are down,
and all four Diamond pilots slam their engines into full
afterburner. At 250 knots and only 150 feet above ground
level, we are flying in one of our tightest formations.

We prepare to start the loop from level flight, in a very
narrow speed-band, so we can make it over the top in our

"dirty" configuration without damaging the landing gear doors. In the Dirty Loop – "dirty" is when the jets' landing gear are down – we're working with a very tight entry airspeed tolerance due to the physical limits of the landing gear doors in the airstream. Too fast and the doors will rip off, but just a few knots slower and the extra drag will reduce the airspeed needed to complete the loop at the top.

Everything has to be just right to safely finish the maneuver.

With full afterburner, the jets accelerate extremely quickly, so we immediately pull back on our sticks. "Up we go," I say, again in rhythmic cadence. "A little more pulllll." We all pull on our sticks on the "G" in the word "go" and keep pulling back until the last "L" sound in the word "pull."

All of a sudden, just as we're reaching pure vertical, I hear and feel, "BAM!... BAM!" I'm getting stalls on my right engine, which sounds like someone hitting the side of the airplane with a sledgehammer.

Immediately, my wingmen recognize an abrupt deceleration of my aircraft and chime up, "Jack is clear, JD is clear, Pepper is clear," as they all move a few feet away from my airplane.

Now we are going straight up. I only have one of my two engines running at full power, while the engine that had been stalling is now pulled back to idle, per the Navy's *boldface* emergency procedures for the F/A-18. Airspeed is dropping fast.

Fortunately for us, our team had discussed the possibility of losing an engine during critical flight regimes such as the Diamond Dirty Loop and Diamond takeoffs.

In fact, we had been concerned enough about what would happen in the Dirty Loop that the Slot pilot and I flew a dozen runs in the F/A-18 simulator between show seasons to see what would happen when an engine failed. We found that by keeping the good engine in full afterburner longer, we had enough thrust – barely – to make it over the top and complete the loop.

However, the wingmen would not be able to stay in close formation due to the significantly degraded engine performance. They would be able to follow in their clear airspace a few feet further from the Boss's aircraft.

Once I safely completed the loop on one engine, I left the rest of the team orbiting over the desert conserving fuel while I landed to perform a "Hot Seat" with the spare jet. "Hot Seat" is when you get into an airplane that is already running having been started by the ground crew. The team practiced these maneuvers like a NASCAR team practices pit stops. When doing an air show over the field, you could often land, taxi in, unstrap out of one jet and strap into the new jet, and takeoff, all within five minutes. Sometimes, only missing one maneuver of the show sequence.

Since we had a contingency plan for what we knew could go wrong – in this case, the loss of an engine – we knew what we needed to do, and it worked out well. The Blue Angels safely perform the Dirty Loop and other maneuvers because of excellent contingency planning: thinking ahead and planning for every problem we could imagine.

Contingency planning is a crucial aspect of the strategic planning cycle. In the military, we had a saying that "Plans only last as long as first contact with the enemy." Therefore, all of our plans have sequels and branches to deal with crises when they arise.

As with inspirational strategic planning, battle rhythm is the key to contingency planning. It allows the team to execute to their very best ability in order to handle situations when they go wrong, and it provides mechanisms for adapting the plan and moving forward.

Sequels and Branches

Well-developed contingency planning involves preparing for both the logical next steps, or *sequels*, and planned reactions to potential changes in the environment, or *branches*. Because the enemy, the marketplace, and your competitors have a vote in what happens, cultures of excellence do not blindly follow their plans when facts on the ground change. They have plans in place for many of those possibilities of change.

> *World-class teams must consider possibilities of what could occur and prepare themselves for those contingencies.*

A strategic military example of a *branch* would be developing an alternate plan should a third-nation state insert themselves into the affairs between two other nations. A logical *sequel* to a war plan would be how to successfully transition from wartime back to a government run by civil authority.

By working out as many sequels and branches as your team or organization can imagine, you will be better prepared to work in tandem to solve the problems in real time. Even though you cannot come up with every single issue that could arise, working through as many as possible will give your team more tools to use for those surprises, or crises, as they happen.

Cultures of excellence ingrain contingency planning into their everyday activities. Everyone in the organization pays attention to potential "what ifs." The CEO thinks about moves a competitor could make. Engineers think about alternative designs in case an existing design fails. Purchasing staff has an alternate source if something happens to a key supplier.

Fighter pilots take pride in knowing what they will do when their jets are on fire, when they lose an engine, or when they are shot in midair. They almost look forward to the chance to prove themselves in a real emergency – almost.

Multi-Level Planning

My contingency planning experience ranges from global strategic military contingency planning during the Iraq War to consulting with U.S. companies competing for a multi-billion dollar contract with multiple competitors. In each instance, those organizations that win have cultures that efficiently execute the contingency planning processes in a methodical, effective manner.

Regardless of the level of planning—operational or tactical—preparing for contingencies involves a cycle of planning. Cultures of excellence assess possibilities and examine risk exposure, and then propose courses of action to mitigate these possibilities. They ultimately select a course of action that is affordable in both cash and time.

At the operational level, they look at everything from natural disasters, such as hurricanes, that could disrupt their supply chain. At the tactical level, these winning organizations have a culture that demands the review of all the "what if" scenarios before going into a business meeting.

Courses of action must work as seamlessly as possible with the organization's mission and bring everyone on the team onboard in vertical alignment. Passion, free will and focus can inform and energize the process.

Organizations and companies that fail to consider the contingencies will be vulnerable to their competition. For example:

- Your competitor could introduce a new line of business, and you have no new products in development.

- You could fall behind on orders when a key product component is unavailable, while your competitor who planned ahead, gained significant market share and goodwill because of their ability to continue to operate.

- You also could find yourself on the defensive in a business negotiation if you had not prepared for exploiting all the possibilities that would keep you in the driver's seat instead of having to react to the moves coming from the other side of the table.

My experiences as a fighter pilot taught me that in air-to-air combat, the pilot who had a solid plan of attack before engaging the enemy fighter could drive the fight, placing the opponent at a serious disadvantage. Even more importantly, if he had thought through all of the possible maneuvers the opponent could use, our pilot could then effectively counter any possible dog-fighting maneuvers in order to come out the victor.

The Never-Ending Process

Contingency planning is both a science and an art. The U.S. military has volumes of publications and many schools dedicated to the methodologies of contingency planning. No one does it better. Many of those resources are available to you in unclassified documents you can find on the Internet.

Much like our military, world-class organizations that consistently win have a culture of contingency planning that permeates all levels of the organization.

Like strategy, contingency planning needs to be a never-ending process. Contingency planning is key to developing the inspirational strategy, since preparing for contingencies helps your team learn to deal with every possible situation you can imagine.

Pick a frequency – once a month, once a quarter, or biennially – that makes sense for your organizational or corporate strategic planning. Top organizations develop a methodical process that covers strategic, operational and tactical goals, reviews the facts, makes assumptions about the unknowns, and then develop contingency plans based on the best information they have available at that time. Then on a periodic basis, they review the contingency plans to ensure the goals, facts, and assumptions are still valid and adjust accordingly.

Contingency Planning: The Impact

The best organizations I have worked with all have cultures of excellence that promote thorough planning and preparation at every level. When a new member joins, they are not only indoctrinated with an inspirational mission and strategic plans to help achieve their goals, they also are passionate about being prepared for every contingency.

Cultures focused on driving the strategy and encouraging the use of free will while looking for new and better ways to effectively handle contingencies regardless of level, size or scope consistently perform better than their peers that do not.

World-class organizations that leverage contingency planning embody high levels of efficiency, which is awe-inspiring to all who witness it. When organizations know what can happen and have prepared for those possibilities, they can deal with problems that arise without compromising safety or excellence.

By striving for efficient and thorough contingency planning, businesses demonstrate to the public accountability and responsibility for their actions. They generate confidence that they can continue to drive the fight through any circumstance.

Boldface Emergency Procedures

Naval aviators have learned over time that there are some contingencies that require emergency procedures and immediate action. The time-sensitive nature of these malfunctions are such that, there is no time to break out a flight manual and look up the required steps. Emergencies such as cockpit fires, engine fires, engine stalls, and loss of control all fit into this category.

Similarly, organizations with cultures of excellence also have boldface procedures for the most time-critical events. Some are very tactical in nature and are mandated by law, such as how to handle a fire or a chemical spill within a factory space. Others are more strategic, such as how to adjust to disruptions in a supply chain by either a man-made or natural disaster.

Memorized, practiced and tested emergency procedures, reacting to changes in the market, competitive landscape or a physical disaster are why the best teams seem to get through tough times.

These teams have the same cool, collected outward demeanor as a fighter pilot in an emergency. That cool outward appearance, coupled with a well-thought-out public affairs plan to both internal and external audiences, is why they always seem to have the public trust. They always look like they know what they are doing!

Points to Remember

1. Contingency planning is an important component of any inspirational strategic plan, and is a never-ending process.

2. World-class contingency plans include as many sequels and branches as are needed to cover the likely follow-on requirements and changes in the environment.

3. An important result of good contingency planning is that the organization or company earns the trust of customers, clients, vendors, shareholders, and the community.

4. Boldface emergency procedures are those well-thought-out and practiced responses to predicted disasters that enhance resilience, and engender a sense of confidence both internal and external to the organization.

Chair Flying Exercise

Visualize your organization's process of acquiring business, creating the product or service, and delivering the product or service to a happy customer. Write down all of the steps that are involved. Next to each step, write down all of the outside organizations and people who are involved in the delivery of your product or service – vendors, manufacturers, and bankers. Think about every single system that your product or service uses. Who are all of the people who touch your process of delivery? What are all of the systems you need to work in tandem – electricity, telephone, trucking companies, mail service?

Now close your eyes and imagine a severe storm – a freak flash flood, a huge tornado ripping through town, a train derailment. How are each of those people, each of those processes, each of those systems that come into contact with your product or service affected by the severity?

At the operational level, do you consider natural disasters, such as hurricanes, floods, fires and pandemics that could disrupt your supply chain? At what level, does your company aggressively plan for contingencies that disrupt the market place?

At the tactical level, does your organization have a culture that demands the review of all the "what ifs" before going into a business meeting? Does your team map all of the conceivable possibilities of where the discussion or negotiations could go?

If not, imagine your planning process. How soon in the planning process do you want these questions asked? Where can you insert these questions? Who would you want in charge of asking the questions? What would you like your contingency process to look like? What does the end result look like? Who do you need to help you reach this vision?

For the scenarios above, has your team developed a set of boldface procedures? Have all the individuals who need to take immediate action, should those scenarios occur, committed the boldface procedures to memory? Have they been tested in a realistic training scenario to ensure they know how to react should that incident occur? Do you have a review process to periodically review "what ifs" and to fine-tune the immediate action responses to those "what ifs?"

"The landing gear coming up at the start of the Diamond Takeoff Loop. The Blue Angels learned about 9-11 while performing a similar takeoff loop in practice."

Photo By Bernard Zee ©

Chapter 7:

Crisis Planning for the Unexpected

Imagining the Unimaginable

I remember every detail.

I was leading the Blue Angels in a perfect Diamond Formation on a crisp, clear morning over our home base in Pensacola, FL. We were in the middle of a takeoff loop when our Blue Angel's Maintenance Officer emphatically and professionally bellowed into the air show frequency.

"Knock it off, knock it off. Boss, you've got to land now."

While our maintenance crew is an important and integral part of the air show, they rarely – if ever – jump onto our air show frequency to order us to land.

The day was September 11, 2001.

Every American remembers where he or she was during 9-11. I will never forget that feeling of amazing freedom turning into a moment of crisis when the decision was made to shut down America's airspace. Anything flying except NORAD-controlled aircraft was instructed to land immediately.

From the tone of our Maintenance Officer's voice, I realized that something was really wrong.

When we landed our jets and turned on the news, we heard the unfolding story of our nation under attack. It was an unexpected shock, so we did not have a contingency plan for this situation. However, we did have plans to deal with crises.

Contingency planning is for the things you know could happen, while crisis planning is a specific subset of contingency planning that provides a methodology and a starting point to respond to those events that happen which you could not have reasonably predicted.

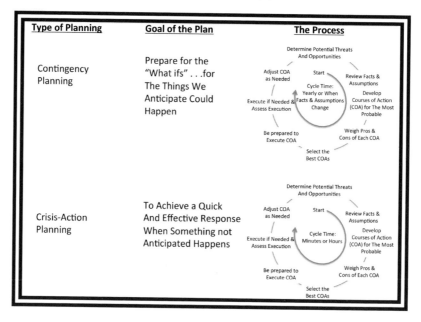

In any organization, contingency planning covers a wide range of potential events. I define these as the events that a manager or leader might reasonably worry about, like an engine failure on a jet, the introduction of a new product by a competitor, or an earthquake interrupting production at a factory in California.

A crisis, however, is on a different scale — the once-in-a-decade or once-in-a-career events that change everything.

Crisis Planning: It's the Process, Stupid

Contingency plans are well-thought-out plans to address specific issues. World-class organizations have instilled a process for creating contingencies into the DNA or the culture of their organizations.

Crisis planning mirrors the process of contingency planning, but in a much more compressed, real-time manner. Crisis planning involves developing and rallying the capability of the team to pull together and deal, by means of a clear and delineated process, with things that go wrong which nobody could have anticipated.

One way to prepare for the unknown is to explore what other organizations have done in various crises. You should look not only at their actions in response to the crisis, but also their process in reaching those difficult action-oriented decisions.

When organizations look at crises that have happened in the past, they can see how, in some cases, the response went relatively well, and in other cases, not so well. This allows your team to examine the reasons why crisis response processes either worked or did not. In either case, lessons learned could aid response capability and enhance preparedness levels for crises that might occur in the future.

The more comprehensive your crisis-action planning process, the more unpredictable events it will be able to cover. Crises should be examined from the standpoint of scope: The size of the population affected, the consequences of the crisis, and how to best mitigate the crisis.

When examining what crisis-action planning processes you need, an organization must consider the types of crises that might arise so as to come up with a process that can handle the magnitude of possibilities. Nations must consider the possibilities of every type of crisis from natural disasters to political uprisings, from pandemics to acts of terrorism, from power outages to disruptions to our technological way of life.

Each type of crisis is a distinct possibility, and each would result in widespread consequences and repercussions. Having been part of our homeland defense team at NORAD and NORTHCOM, I can tell you that they continually refine their processes to improve their crisis response capacity.

The key to successfully weathering any situation is to have a process for responding to a crisis – any crisis. Even though the exact scenario you may face will vary, having a process in place that covers the "worst case" equips everyone with the skills needed to navigate when all the usual sign posts are gone.

Developing a Crisis-Action Process

Like contingency planning, the crisis planning process is both an art and a science. Again, the U.S. military has volumes of manuals and schools dedicated to perfecting the trade.

It is key to stress the importance of having a process that:

- Sets immediate goals,
- Gathers facts,
- Develops assumptions, and
- Maximizes communication both internally to decision-makers and those in the field and, externally to critical audiences that could include clients, the media and the public at large.

The decision makers will then take action as the process continues to provide updated information in a cyclic rhythm.

The crisis is over when you are driving the fight and no longer reacting to unanticipated events.

As fighter pilots, Blue Angels, and TOPGUN instructors, we learned the importance of taking the same steps each time we executed a mission, so that we created a kind of muscle memory—easily repeatable steps every time, even when something out of the ordinary happened. Additionally, we learned the value of mission-type orders, which focus on the ultimate goal.

When something that is so far out of the ordinary occurs, knowing what the ultimate mission is will help you make decisions, even if communication is severed to your base – or your boss. This is how we plan to operate in combat if communications are cut—everyone knows the big picture, the mission and the goals, and then uses their best judgment to guide their actions.

The Performance Triad – passion, focus, and free will – must be at work.

Determine Your Process, Then Execute

Like the elite organizations, your team will need to develop an easy-to-execute, repeatable process that will work under the most stressful scenarios. This process gives your organization a backbone for its response that will work across numerous unforeseen events.

When you have the same process, team members can become very familiar with it, and it becomes part of the team's battle rhythm. Your plan must have:

- Immediate-action items,

- Boldface plans, that are integral parts of the process, and

- Emphasize and enhance communications abilities, both internally among the team and externally, with other organizations that might need to be brought to bear in the event of a crisis.

The most vital part of crisis communications is keeping the conduit open between the decision makers and other people who are working to mitigate the crisis. When that communication is severed, you must arm those in the field with mission-type orders that allow them to make the best decisions they can, based on what they see.

You must create a process, and then trust The Performance Triad to work.

To fill out your crisis-action process, pre-identify roles and responsibilities among the team. Ask yourself, "What is the problem, and what is the mission?" Then delegate roles and duties that are appropriate for your organization. Brainstorm as many assumptions as possible regarding what your organization will need to do to deal with a given crisis, both at its outset and as the crisis unfolds.

Based on these assumptions, determine courses of action, and then make sure that your team will be able to execute these plans. Reassess your plan and keep it up-to-date by obtaining new information wherever and whenever possible, and as necessary, re-plan.

Never neglect the cycle of review, because things are always changing, and there is sure to be new information that could factor into any given contingency.

Again, the process should tie in with the passion, commitment and motivation of the whole team. Trust within the team in a crisis is more important than ever. Just like a fighter pilot in combat with inoperable communication gear, you need to believe that others will be making the right decisions and continuing to work together, no matter what.

Once you have the process, you must be able to execute it. That is where practicing how you are going to handle a crisis is tremendously important. It is one thing to have plans, but it is another thing to be able to execute them. Executing plans with efficiency is where deliberate practice comes in.

Organizations with high-risk elements—running an oil refinery, for instance—make practice routines as authentic as possible, often with physical drills and simulations. All organizations, even those with less high-risk potential, will always benefit from a simpler walk-through approach—periodically repeated so everyone has an idea of their role.

Organizations must answer these three key questions:

1. Who are the decision makers?

2. How will these decision makers receive information to make decisions in real-time?

3. How will the team develop a crisis communications procedure in which each team member will know

his or her roles and responsibilities when something unexpected happens?

Since each unforeseen possibility will be different, exercising a crisis-action planning process requires tremendous flexibility in communications and a high degree of trust among team members. This is critical not just for physical catastrophes but also for financial shifts, changes in competitive landscape, and the rise of new paradigms.

As a world-class organization, the Blue Angels strives to excel at crisis management, using the principles described above: Developing the process and facilitating communication in critical, holistic alignment.

The ultimate goal of a well-executed crisis action plan is not only to deal effectively with the crisis, but also to facilitate a coming-together of people to focus their passion and free will to excel at executing in the new environment.

Post 9-11: Resilience

The 9-11 attacks were a crisis nobody could have foreseen. The Blues' battle rhythm was completely disrupted – air shows were cancelled for security reasons for more than a month.

We continued to perform practice demonstrations at our home base after the attacks, but the intensity was missing.

Instead of spending a lot of time together as a team on the road, we spent more time at home with our families. Normally that would be a good thing, but it created a significant change to our battle rhythm and routine.

We found the passion and focus needed to perform at a world-class level was hard to muster, and we started making mistakes in practice. The Blues had the resiliency to pull back together because of the culture of excellence developing over the years as well as our passion for what we do and our commitment to one another as a team.

How did we do that? We kept communicating, and because of our tight alignment as a team, we had already developed excellent protocols for communication on which we could draw during the crisis. A dedication to communication throughout a crisis will keep alive people's passion for the job and their commitment to the team.

Because of our crisis action process, when the call finally came to do another show, we were able to get back on track by developing an inspirational strategic plan with a theme of "Dedicated to Freedom." We then took the unprecedented step of taking the team to our off-season, winter training facility in El Centro, California to refocus.

After weeks of cancellations, the Blue Angels' very first show following 9-11 was in Alliance, TX. For the Blues and the audience, it will go down as one of the most memorable patriotic events ever.

Everything worked. Even the weather was in our favor: We had a beautiful and clear Texas sky with almost no wind. Even better, we had an awesome crowd. We were heartened by the response of the audience, their powerful surge of patriotism and their passion to connect with us.

I will never forget, after our walk-back, the woman in the crowd line who hugged me and expressed her appreciation for the military and her gratitude to the team and me for everything we stood for.

Thanks to the good old Texas spirit portrayed by everyone in Alliance, I realized that the nation was going to be okay. It was resilient. That's how you like a crisis to end: with a confident, forward-looking attitude.

Points to Remember

1. Contingency planning is for the things you know could happen, while crisis planning is a specific subset of contingency planning to respond to those events that happen which you could not have reasonably predicted.

2. Contingency planning relies on the "what" of your plan, while crisis planning focuses on the "how" of your plan.

3. Cultures of excellence create a process that identifies who the decision makers will be during the crisis,

how they will receive information in real-time, and
how they will communicate back to the team.

4. All team members, not just the key decision makers,
    need to understand the plan so they can execute
    even if they are unable to communicate with the
    leadership.

Chair Flying Exercise

Remember back to where you were during the attacks
of September 11, 2001. Where were you? What were you
doing? Who was the first person you tried to contact to
see if they were OK, and to tell them you were OK? What
issues did you face in making that contact? How did you
feel until you could reach them? Did you wish you had a
plan in place for such an attack? What is your plan today
to contact that person you immediately tried to contact on
9-11?

Now take those thoughts and feelings to your current organization. Who would you need to contact to ensure that
your organization was still intact and able to run smoothly?
What process do you have in place to create contingency
plans? How could you best speed up that process to
address a crisis? Ask yourself – and your team – How do
you shave off 20 percent of the time it takes to make a plan
and execute it? How can you shave 50 percent of the time?
90 percent?

"Preparing to brief an air show, like a business meeting, requires focus."

Photo By Trent Kalp [©]

"This scene is minutes before an air show brief where all distractions will be eliminated and everyone will be totally in the moment as the pilots and support crew visualize their roles throughout the entire air show sequence together."

Photo By Trent Kalp [©]

Chapter 8:
The Key to Continuous Improvement

Succeeding on Purpose

All of the officers—pilots and support crew—are around our conference table, facing each other. The Boss is at the head of the table. The room is filled with historic memorabilia, pictures, trophies, and reminders of the traditions of excellence we were given the privilege to uphold. The officers are silent waiting for the briefing to begin.

Cell phones are to be turned off. We can only use our eyes, ears, and minds.

We are in the ready-room before an air show; the whole team is present with passion, focus and free will to make this the best flight ever.

The mood is very upbeat and lighthearted until about 30 seconds before the top of the hour. Then dead silence as the chair flying exercise begins.

At exactly the top of the hour, I say, "Admin." The Lead Solo pilot, #5, who is also the Operations Officer, makes some very brief administrative remarks. Then it is time to get down to business.

"We are parked in reverse order for a reverse walkdown," I tell the group, as we begin our visualization, or chair flying, exercise. "We will start up on channels 8, 9 and 18… Take of checks will be done in the chocks…When the Solos are ready, we will switch channel 16 in com 2."

"We'll be cleared for takeoff with a winds check," I say as we run down the standard procedures. "Check your parking brake off, check your trim set. Maneuver: Diamond Burner Half Cuban Eight, with a left turnout. The Solos will be in from the right with the section go.

"Number Five's Dirty Roll on takeoff and Number Six's low-transition, high-performance climb to Split S. The Diamond will be in from the right with the Diamond 360. Solos will be in with the opposing Knife Edge. Diamond will be in from the right with the Diamond Roll. Solos will be in the with the opposing inverted."

I continue the briefing all the way through to shutting down the aircraft, going to the crowd line. No step in the process is too small or insignificant to review. We even discuss exactly when and where we are going to do the debrief after the air show.

We finish our general brief by reciting one of the emergency action procedures for the treasured Blue Angel F/A-18 fighter jet. To keep us all on our toes, our #3 wingman would randomly pick one of the 100+ emergency scenarios, and we would all recite the immediate action steps from rote memory. That is our boldface.

Training is not just learning how to do your job; it also includes throwing in different problems so you also learn how to react to the unusual while rehearsing the usual. World-class organizations never let a practice go without throwing a wrench in the plan to learn how team members will react when things are not perfect.

The Blue Angels conducted their entire brief from memory with no note cards. The only thing we used were satellite imagery of the show site and surrounding areas with our checkpoints drawn on them. Other than the Boss – me – there was complete silence as the pilots crouched in their chairs to chair fly the maneuvers, eyes closed, visualizing how it was going to happen.

You would think that this was one of the first times we were going through it, because it was so detailed. However, this was the same brief I gave when I started as a brand-new Boss two years earlier. Now I am a seasoned Boss for this team's very last show.

We briefed the overall air show as a group with all the officers, including Diamond pilots, the Solo pilots, the Fat Albert aircrew and all our support officers. At the end of the overall brief, we each would state what our specific goal was for that day. Our mood was upbeat, but also serious.

We were about to do an air show in front of thousands of fans, often with very challenging environmental conditions such as winds, clouds, turbulence and precipitation.

Following the brief, we kept to ourselves. We were getting into the zone, visualizing and warming up our muscle memory.

We would go to maintenance control and sign for the aircraft, drive out to the show line, and wait for our turn to perform. The timing was always such that the F/A-18 demo pilots would walk out to their F/A-18 Blue Angel aircraft just as the Marines were revving up Fat Albert – our C-130 cargo plane – to start their demo.

Finally, when it was our turn, we would form up in front of the jets, perform our walk down, and smartly climb in, all in cadence with the narrator's announcement. It was then time to execute. The briefing ritual was always the same, whether in practice or at an actual air show.

After completing the demo, we would finish by smartly shutting down the aircraft in unison, opening the aircraft canopy, removing our helmets, then dismounting the aircraft. We would quickly debrief maintenance on the aircraft systems, write up any discrepancies, and then sign the aircraft back over to them.

After the first show of the season, our practices at our home field were open to the public. Even on those occasions we would try to make everything the same as any air show.

We would spend as much time as we could at the crowd line, signing autographs and chatting with the audience. Eventually, we would break away and return to the ready-room to debrief.

Again, the routine was the same regardless of whether it was a practice or an actual air show. We would again become very serious. Starting with me, the Boss, we would each quickly review the important debrief points of the various maneuvers and discuss our individual specific goals as to how we did achieving them.

Additionally, we would each discuss *safeties*. A safety was anything we may have done that did not comply with the Blue Angels' standard operating procedures. If the safety was considered a violation of a rule, we would pay $5 to our recreation fund.

Another important rule of the Blues' debriefing was "No Rank." The Boss, also the team's commanding officer, even though he is one or two levels of rank above the rest of the team, must be open to criticism to empower the whole group to really dig into the details of what they can do better.

Learning is best if it is more than just a mental exercise. It needs to become part of each individual team member's routine, and part of the organization's way of doing business. In Naval Aviation, this is accomplished through constant *deliberate practice*. Drills are obviously important in sports, but also in business.

For instance, IT organizations have learned how important it can be to practice disaster recovery. To ensure corporate data is safe, IT operations may occasionally be transferred temporarily to a remote location to prove that it could be done smoothly if ever required by real events. Or, occasionally, businesses will simulate challenges of operating under emergency conditions or sourcing new suppliers to deal with sudden supply chain disruptions.

Whatever it is, the exercise should be relevant and realistic – and it should test the skill and capabilities of as many parts of the organization as possible. Done well, it can become not merely something people have to do, but something they want to do because it allows them to test their skills to the limit and to achieve a shared goal together.

Developing a Deliberate Training Plan

U.S. Navy Photo

U.S. Navy Photo

"The Solos practice their individual take-off maneuvers before putting them together as a section."

Photo By Bernard Zee ©

Just as Coach Wooden would start with the basics of the proper way to put on socks and lace up shoes, the Blues started every new show season with the basics, then built up to the air show.

This deliberate training plan was designed to break down the air show maneuvers into their basic elements, so basic, in fact, that to the outside observer they almost seemed ridiculously simple for hard-core, seasoned fighter pilots.

These elements included: (1) turning the smoke on and off in unison, (2) taxiing together in precise formation on the ground, (3) making basic turns, (4) putting the speed brakes out and in at the same time, and (4) putting the landing gear down and raising them at the same time. All these elements seem very simple and have been accomplished thousands of times, but never before have they needed to be done with such precision, in such tight formation, as for Blue Angels air show maneuvers.

Paying attention to details and consistently mastering them can also be critical in business. For example, the way customers are greeted and treated by a retailer can set a consistent tone that assures customers they are in the right place and doing business with competent, capable people.

For us, the training routine was intentionally designed to be close to the regular routine of an air show. It was part of the way we lived as members of the Blues. Because everyone knew its importance, the winter training mindset revolved around total dedication to getting ready for the show. It ensured that distractions were minimized and that the entire team was prepared on all levels: physically, spiritually, and emotionally.

In cultures of excellence, training and planning are not conducted one time, nor are they seasonal. Rather, they are continuous, ongoing processes that are constantly and consistently improved.

Briefing and Debriefing – a Critical Element of Focus

A hallmark of a culture of excellence is the thoroughness and effectiveness of their post-mission debrief.
Photo By Trent Kalp©

Everything the Blue Angels do in practice is recorded and debriefed as part of training. The key to learning the demo in such a short period of time and being able to execute to a tremendously high level was the briefing and debriefing process. That's a great takeaway for any organization.

In the ready-room, team members go through the briefing process before a demo and the debriefing process afterward, which include discussions on execution, specific goals for maneuvers, specific elements for which each pilot will be responsible, and offering support across the board for everyone's shared responsibilities.

Briefing and debriefing are done whether it is practice, the first show, or the 300th show. The process throughout is always the same. When you are well briefed and then held accountable through debriefing, you know what you are doing, and you build on what you know.

In my experience, debriefing stands out as a key differentiator between those organizations that have a culture of excellence, and those that do not. Organizations that lack passion, focus and free will are the ones where people are too tired after an event. They don't want to be held accountable. They are embarrassed if they made mistakes. In contrast, those that excel cannot wait to debrief to see where they could do better next time.

The debriefing is where real learning and improvement come from.

Honesty as Key

The "No Rank" and the "Five Dollar Rule" help keep true honesty alive in the briefing and debriefing process of the Blue Angels.

During debriefing, everyone in the team figuratively takes off his or her rank insignia. We all know each other's rank, but the figurative action symbolically says that we are all equally prepared to listen and learn. When the flight demonstration team returns from a practice to talk about whether they achieved specific goals, the senior officers must be willing to take debriefs from subordinates as gracefully as the subordinates take debriefs from those more senior.

It is a time when passion, free will and focus are on full display. If, as a Blue Angels team member, you did something wrong or deviated from a standard operating procedure, you would have to call it on yourself during debriefing. If you did not call yourself out on your mistake, someone else would call it for you, and then you would have to put five dollars in the kitty. The Five Dollar Rule is a good-natured way of keeping everybody honest.

The only way for anybody, regardless of rank, to improve in executing their mission is to understand what can be done better and how to do it better.

The "No Rank" Debrief Culture

When consulting for businesses, I have noticed that people are often afraid to tell the emperor that he has no clothes.

"No Rank" can serve as a highly useful methodology to foster cultures of excellence. Performance is maximized when people – no matter what their position of authority – understand what they have done wrong and can then correct it. "No Rank," epitomized by open and honest communication, is a necessary element in high-end business culture, both building it and maintaining it.

Leaders cannot be afraid to open up to their team members, or to expose their faults. In fact, they must. If a leader is afraid to expose his or herself, then they are not ready to lead a culture of excellence.

Points to Remember

1. Deliberate Training Plans start with the basics, and pay great attention to details so that each member of the team develops the proper muscle memory over time so that they consistently and methodically master their skills.

2. Demos and drills that are relevant and realistic are an important part of creating a system for continuous improvement.

3. Briefing and debriefing are imperative to develop a culture of excellence that embraces continuous improvement.

4. Removing rank, acknowledging errors and refusing to accept the status quo are important rules for real continuous improvement.

Chair Flying Exercise

Think of a process that is central to your organization's success. It can be your website where you take the majority of your orders and make the most money. It can be the long, arduous process of earning governmental approval for a new medical device. It can even be an artistic process.

Do you do an annual run-through of this key process? If you do, do you routinely throw a wrench into the plan to see how the team reacts? How much feedback do you give your team? How often is the feedback? If you do not have a run-through or do not test the team on their reactions to problems, why don't you? How can you remove those obstacles, so that you can make this a part of your business processes?

Imagine now that you are having a realistic practice run-through of this key process. Who is involved? Who is not involved? Why are they not involved – do you have staff who are not involved with the central process of your organization? If so why aren't they involved? Are you missing out on capturing all of the passion, free will and focus available in your organization? When was the last time someone in your organization critiqued your performance?

In this run-through that you are visualizing, what problems can you throw into the mix? How do you think your team will react? How would you like them to react? Do you have some issues you need to address in your organization before you would feel comfortable having a run-through or tossing in certain issues? How can you set the stage to develop a continuous improvement process and make it a staple in your regular business plan? If you already have a plan like this, how can you improve it? What other parts of your organization could benefit from a deliberate training program?

Think of a typical meeting in your organization. Compare it to how the Blue Angels approach every meeting. Are people held accountable to be there on time? Is everyone focused or are they on their smart phones or tablets taking care of other business?

When your organization is preparing for an event, whether in business such as a meeting with a client, or a sports team heading to a game, do you brief and practice as close to the real thing as possible? Does each player have a specific goal they are trying to achieve? Do you take the time to debrief afterwards on what could be done better next time? If you do, you are on your way to achieving a culture of excellence.

"Your team's culture of excellence designed to balance passion, free will and focus will enable them to triumphantly return with style from every mission ready to win again! An F/A-18 Hornet, at night, catching an aircraft carrier arresting wire and decelerating from 150 knots to zero in just a few hundred feet. The U.S. Navy culture of excellence does it better than anyone else."

U.S. Navy Photo Taken By MC3 Chad R. Erdmann

Section 3:

Creating A Winning Legacy -

How to Sustain the Culture to Win

"Hanging on the blades," as naval aviators say, at only 230 knots, I am throttled back trying to save fuel in my F/A-18. It is a pitch black stormy December night over the Mediterranean Sea.

I can feel a few Gs in my shallow turns and a lot of pride. The training exercise was executed perfectly so far. The CATSHOT was smooth. Navigating my craft through bad weather and disorientating Saint Elmo's Fire dancing all over my canopy with my instruments, using my years of experience, is rewarding.

Now comes the hard part – slowing down to a mere 150 knots and landing my 33,000-pound aircraft on about 500 feet of runway.

It is nearly winter, and the Mistral Winds south of France are howling. The carrier's flight deck is pitching significantly tonight. I have planned my fuel to arrive at the flight deck with just the right amount to give me the best chance to get aboard. However, as well as I have planned, there are still many things that are out of my control.

Even though I see the visual landing aid, the *meatball*, on the flight deck that normally tells me I am coming in at just the right angle, I am going to have to rely on specially trained pilots, known as landing signal officers (LSO). They are standing on the flight deck, just to the left of the landing area, ready to talk me down.

The deck is pitching so much that the meatball is unreliable. Fighter jets usually only have enough fuel for two, maybe three attempts to land before they have to go up and plug into a tanker aircraft to get more fuel. I have already heard the LSO's command several of my fellow pilots to wave off their approaches as the flight deck gyrations and their aircraft were out of phase with each other.

They were waved off, because if they landed, they were in danger of significantly damaging their aircraft which could not only jeopardizes their own personal safety and the integrity of the aircraft, but also prevent the rest of the air wing from recovering.

If things go well, the LSOs and I will be in synch, I will respond to their commands giving them exactly what they are asking me to do with my aircraft, I will grab the third wire with my airplane's tailhook. I will follow the standard procedure of going to full power as soon as I land, in case I miss all the wires and bolter.

Then all I have to do is trust that I caught the wire and that the aircraft carrier crew have done their job properly so the airplane and the deck are in perfect working order. Otherwise, up I go, back into the night sky to try again. Hopefully, I will have enough fuel.

While I may be the only pilot in the F/A-18, I am not alone. It takes the whole team to get me up and bring me down again – safely.

On the deck of a carrier, there is no substitute for excellence. The flight deck is one of the most consistently demanding, dangerous places to work in the world.

The carrier and the air wing must always be ready to defend the country. Therefore, flight operations are conducted day and night in the worst weather and in every extreme of climate.

At the same time, the majority of the crew servicing, launching, and recovering the aircraft are just out of high school. People, who in most civilian organizations would be confined to entry-level roles with little responsibility, are trained and conditioned to accomplish things as a team that are remarkable.

Over time, the Navy has developed an amazing safety record in flight deck operations. It has accomplished this by spending a lot of time and effort preparing the team; garnering feedback and learning lessons throughout the execution of duties; and remembering to stay focused long after the mission in front of them is over.

We always have another mission. Let's look to the future.

"Fat Albert, Part of the Blue Angel Legacy."

Photo by Toru EBISAWA ©

Chapter 9:
Developing Your Organization's Mystique

My bags were barely unpacked after returning from my first overseas deployment on the USS Coral Sea with my squadron – the VFA-131 Wildcats – when I got the call. I remember my boss telling me, "Congrats, Ice, you're headed to the TOPGUN Power Projection Course. Represent us well."

Next thing I knew, my bags were packed and my sister-squadron wingman for that course, Lumpy, and I were flying across country to Miramar, CA, to meet the best fighter pilots in the world and represent our squadrons. I was prepared to absorb as much as possible from the tactical lectures and airborne lessons delivered by the legendary instructors at TOPGUN.

Even before the flying commenced, I was blown away by how impressive these guys were.

The way the TOPGUN instructors stood in front of the class and delivered their material was awe-inspiring.

It still ranks in my mind as the best delivery I have ever witnessed. I had never seen that level of presentation before, and I haven't seen its equal since, not even in the numerous Four-Star and Presidential-level presentations I have witnessed.

Polished presentations are a trademark of TOPGUN. The confidence the TOPGUN instructors displayed was unbelievable. They knew the material so well that they seldom looked at their slides, yet made blind transitions from one to the next. It was an art form unto itself. Each lecture complemented the next, and they were all perfectly coordinated. Even the handoff between speakers was in total synchronization.

Once again, it was passion, focus and free will in action. Unlike settings in which one person often contradicts what another says, and where presentations are often haphazard or disorganized, the TOPGUN instructors spoke authoritatively and with one voice, demonstrating critical alignment, which every great culture needs. Their persona was such that you had no doubt that these were the best fighter pilots in the world, and the most professional.

After listening to the TOPGUN instructors speak and watching the way they interacted with the crowd, I decided then and there that I wanted to be like those guys.

I have always been a confident person, but when I first arrived at the TOPGUN school, I worried that I might not measure up. I think most people feel that way going in, but once they see how TOPGUN does it and they become a part of it - the magic happens. The synchronization of core values occurs from the beginning.

Later, when I became a TOPGUN instructor myself, it became even more obvious to me why the TOPGUN course and lectures were so synchronized.

Each instructor is responsible for knowing and espousing techniques and procedures for air combat that are standardized. We referred to this as, "the *STAN*." However, they do allow for various instructor techniques so the students can sample different methods for accomplishing critical tasks. The focus of STAN and the free will of technique makes a great combination that makes executing at a very high level as effective as possible.

For a particular weapons employment method for example, once the Instructor Staff agrees to the STAN, that is the way it is. You can always count on your fellow fighter pilot to execute to the STAN. This is critical in combat and equally critical in business.

When I go into organizations as a consultant, it is obvious which businesses have well-defined standards that are clear and understood by all, and those that do not. I learned from my time at TOPGUN that having a culture that knows how to develop and hold people accountable for the STAN is critical for peak performance—another hallmark of a world-class organization.

My experience with the Blue Angels was similar.

As a junior officer, I was fortunate enough to know some of the team, to observe a brief and to get a back seat ride during an actual flight demonstration. I watched them execute. I watched them debrief. I saw how professional the whole team was, not just the pilots, but everyone.

I was amazed by how well they interacted with one another and with other people. And the way they flew was inspiring. There was no doubt that these were among the best pilots around and that the Blues was the best flight demonstration team in the world. The experience convinced me that I really wanted to be a Blue Angel.

When I was fortunate enough to become Boss, I saw what it was that made the Blues tick.

The organization has a core code of what it means to be a Blue Angel. The code is made up of points that range from how the Blues groom and handle themselves as to how they interact with people at the crowd line.

The code also includes how Blue Angels deal with each other in the ready-room. None of these points are written down, but the bottom line is that there is this core code. The code results in high standards, which keep the team at its top level, help project a great image to the public, and keep everyone safe.

TOPGUN and the Blue Angels constitute the best examples of core values instilled into an organization. This has kept them recognized as the world's best-run organizations for a long time. It was the existence of both written and non-written core values, and a commitment to continuously improving execution in everything they did that made these organizations so unique.

TOPGUN's culture of excellence started during the Vietnam War when we had a real world wartime goal – the goal of being able to transfer a lot of knowledge in the shortest period of time, and to get the pilots back to their squadrons quickly. The key concepts are just as relevant today.

Cultures of Excellence: Key Concepts

> ## Enable Free Will

To build a culture of excellence, you must spur entrepreneurship in an organization so that people feel free to reach out and do great things within the bounds they are allowed to do so.

While it is important not to break the rules that you have designed for your organization, and every organization does need some rules, you must also be careful not to err on the side of having too many restrictions. When you over-regulate with too many burdensome rules, you wind up stifling initiative – both that of your team members and in the context of your organization as a whole.

In the military, we often achieve this goal by issuing mission-based orders. The end-goal is specified but not how to get there. And, if there is additional guidance it is usually just in the form of guardrails – do not fly in a certain area, do not use a certain kind of ordnance, etc.

➢ Know Your Limits and When to Adjust Them

Consistently successful teams never forget what got them to that point. They live by their rules, and only adjust those rules by a conscious, mutual decision process on the part of the entire team.

"Exactly at the prescribed (just subsonic) airspeed and altitude limit, although tempting to go even lower and faster, cultures of excellence stay true to the limits they set for themselves."
Photos by Bernard Zee ©

When a team adjusts the rules, everyone must talk about the implications, keeping in mind the overriding mission. They may remember what they are trying to do and their history. In other words, the team needs to review the limits that were previously set and understand why those limits were set in the first place, before making a change.

➤ Look Out for One Another

Pride of membership in something truly special leads to

mutual support and reinforcement, thus furthering and perpetuating the culture of excellence.

Looking out for one another is one of the most necessary, meaningful, and inspiring manifestations of core values in action. Cultures of excellence display a strong sense of *esprit de corps*, through which team members let one another know by word and by deed: "I've got your back."

➤ Watch Out for So-Called "Experts"

Use experts, but don't blindly follow them.

Cultures of excellence know when to tap into experts— but also know to not blindly follow them. After asking for expertise, apply critical thinking to the advice that is given. I often asked former Blue Angel Bosses for advice, but at the end of the day, I was responsible for making the decisions. Their unique insight became valuable to give me ideas and to try to prevent having to learn old lessons over again.

➤ Maintain Holistic Alignment

Leaders need to be in synch with each other on the organizational goals, standards and direction, and present a united front to maintain holistic alignment throughout the organization.

"The Blue Angel Diamond formation is so tight that any move by one individual aerodynamically effects all others. This is a great metaphor that highlights the importance of maintaining alignment at the top of the organization."

U.S. Navy Photo

In the business world, core values of critical alignment and mutual support translate into keeping the senior team — the CEO, CFO, COO and others — all on the same beat. The day-to-day, month-to-month, and year-to-year practice of watching out for one another in holistic alignment contributes to excellence in non-military organizations, just as it contributes to excellence in military organizations.

This is the Blue Angels' "Diamond 360" Metaphor — flying so close that the movement of one, ripples through all the rest. That alignment permeates the entire organization. Organizations only create a culture of excellence when they are aligned both vertically and laterally.

➢ Clean Jets Fly Better

Top-performing organizations always look squared away.

Your organization's underlying mindset permeates throughout the whole organization. Perfect, clean, visible perfection not only is an indication of excellence, it helps to drive it. As a Carrier Group Commander, I flew with all seven of my squadrons. The ones that had the cleanest appearing jets also had the best performing jets. Amazingly, their paperwork was always in order and they never missed deadlines — clean jets do fly better!

Organizations that are squared away administratively – in other words, have clean jets – also perform better . . . and so do the people on the team!

➢ Slower is Faster

Winners are relentless in finding ways to simplify, streamline, and get the job done right the first time in a methodical and predictable way.

Our experience in pursuing our goal at the Blue Angels to reduce the amount of time it took to complete all the maneuvers in the demo, led to our saying, "slower is faster." In practice, we found the process to be counterintuitive. When we tried to just pick up the pace and go from maneuver to maneuver faster, we made mistakes and the demo actually took more time. However, when we focused on precision, simplification, and efficiency of movement, our show times got shorter and the demo looked better. From the cockpit point of view, the quickest demos actually seemed slower. From this vantage point, slower is actually faster!

The Left Echelon Roll: How Tradition and Uniqueness Can Fuel the Relentless Pursuit of Perfection

"The Left Echelon Roll is the most difficult rolling maneuver - a legacy handed down from the very first Blue Angel Team and a key element to the culture of excellence."

Photo by Bernard Zee ©

"Simple and spectacular."
Photo by Bernard Zee ©

The *pain cave*. The *coal mine*. These are the terms the Blue Angels Diamond pilots use when referring to what it feels like when performing a series of maneuvers called the "Fan," the "Left Echelon Roll," and the "Line Abreast Loop."

During winter training and throughout the show season, the Diamond pilots would huddle around the video monitor during the debrief, watching the playback of these particular maneuvers in agony.

Sometimes we wondered why we even put forth so much effort as their graceful appearance masked the amount of skill and practice needed to accomplish them properly. They did not have the pizzazz and thrilling crowd appeal of much more simple-to-perform maneuvers such as a classic "Delta Breakout," which looks like a spectacular bomb burst.

Of the three maneuvers, the Left Echelon Roll is the hardest to perfect.

In fact, tracing history back to 1946, the Blue Angels were the first and only flight demonstration team to have perfected this maneuver. This created a sense of tradition and uniqueness, which became one of the team's inspirations in the continuous pursuit of perfection.

To understand how challenging it is to be safe and have the maneuver look good, imagine yourself as the Number Four wingman.

You are at the very end of an echelon formation where everyone is stacked out to the left side of the Boss – Boss, Number Two, Number Three, and Number Four. You can only see Number Three's airplane and Number Three can only see Number Two's airplane.

To perform the maneuver, the Boss pulls the nose up about 45 degrees above the horizon going 350 knots (400 MPH) and rolls into you. Any deviation caused by a change in the Boss's rate of roll due to even the slightest variations in his control stick pressure or outside factors such as air turbulence will be increasingly accentuated the further out in the formation you are.

You as Number Four are at the end of a whip. Everything must be perfect for the maneuver to look right. The Boss's rate-of-roll must build smoothly and consistently for 90 degrees, maintain the same rate for the next 180 degrees, then consistently slow for the last 90 degrees.

Just the slightest deviation in rate will make the formation look noticeably misaligned.

Meanwhile, the wingman must catch deviations immediately and make adjustments for them smoothly, or the wingmen further out in the formation will have to react in ever-increasing magnitudes to stay in position.

Now imagine doing this maneuver on a turbulent day. Now imagine having to look directly into the sun as you roll, reacting to only the jet just feet in front of you.

It is the most challenging, uncomfortable, unnatural formation to fly – and it takes lots of deliberate practice to get it right. In our case, as with teams before ours, this is when the passion created by the tradition of doing something unique shows its value.

That passion to be unique gave us the persistence necessary to keep trying. This was especially important when our performance had plateaued for days or weeks; and we would look out at the trees through the ready-room window before our preflight brief and see them blowing around wildly. We knew we were in for a lot of turbulence. It was going to be rough.

Every organization should have a chance to "own" something that sets it apart, and helps to strengthen the team.

The Left Echelon Roll may seem a little exotic or unlike the kind of activity performed by most teams and businesses. But every organization has, or should have, a tradition of being able to do something unique that promotes The Performance Triad of every one of your team members.

Maybe it is a milestone for operational efficiency, or a characteristic quality of design or fit and finish. It could even be simple things like a manufacturer not just meeting regulatory requirements but also consistently surpassing them as a way to emphasize and foster excellence.

For the Blues, the Left Echelon Roll wasn't a make-work exercise. It was a process that built our confidence and sense of identity. It stimulated every element of The Performance Triad and it made us fly even better.

Points to Remember

1. Every business and organization needs to have something that is unique – a process, a product, an attitude – that everyone in the company understands, can take pride in and will rally around.

2. A commitment to continuously improving processes and execution of plans throughout your organization is key to becoming a world-class organization.

3. Top performing organizations pay attention to details and it shows with every point of contact, both internally and externally, because "Clean jets fly better."

Visualization

Think about what is unique about your organization or business. Is it your customer service, your product or service quality, your location? How is that unique quality communicated to your employees from top to bottom? What role does each of them play in promoting that unique quality and/or in making sure that quality is indeed top-notch? If some of your staff or coworkers are not involved in the core differentiator of your organization, how can you get them involved?

Visualize what you would like your customers/clients, vendors, employees, shareholders and community to say about you when they are socializing. What does each of those groups of people need to experience and/ or understand about your organization in order to make those comments to their friends and family? What training or encouragement do you need to give your team so that they have the tools to provide the experience and the information to communicate your uniqueness to each of these groups of people?

If you cannot think of a unique quality, or if you are not sure that your unique quality can be sustained, what do you wish was your unique quality? Do you wish that your company's service or product had a different feature? Do you wish that your pricing were more flexible, or more standardized? Do you wish your offerings were more diverse, or more focused? Imagine the perfect organization – one that is efficient, effective, and energized.

Visualize the ideal version of your organization. What do you need to do to make that vision a reality? What decisions need to be made? What information is needed to make those decisions? Who needs to be involved? Where in the process of transforming to the ideal organization can each person in the organization get involved? What are the steps along the way, and the milestones you will pass, that let you know you are headed in the right direction, together?

"The Performance Multiplier Effect is apparent in the Blue Angel Support Team. Passion, free will and focus in every department, not just the pilots in front of the crowd, is a hallmark of a world-class organization."

Photo By Trent Kalp ©

Chapter 10:

The Performance Multiplier Effect

Maximizing the Performance Triangle

L anding on the flight deck of a U.S. aircraft carrier in my F/A-18 Hornet fighter jet, the over 1,000-foot deck looks small and peaceful. Yet after I climb out of the cockpit and walk across the deck, ducking moving propellers and bustling crew members, the deck looks like an endless obstacle course.

Proof that your view of an organization can change dramatically in just a few moments.

Every U.S. Navy Fleet F/A-18 Squadron is assigned the same basic equipment – it operates from a 97,000-ton carrier, each F/A-18 squadron usually has 12 aircraft, 17 pilots, 170 support personnel and associated support equipment. Yet some squadrons seem to always be at the top of any competition or group award, and they are always the most desired when personnel are looking for orders.

Because of this controlled equal-asset environment, the Navy serves as a great Petri dish by which to examine how cultures of excellence develop and how success builds on itself. Some fleet squadrons distinguish themselves as cultures of excellence, and everybody wants to get into these squads. The pilots and support personnel are drawn to them because of their reputation of adhering to the highest quality standards and being great places to work.

People want to be part of a culture of excellence.

After years of studying the best fleet squadrons, I have found that they have developed what I call the Performance Multiplier Effect. They have learned to generate exuberance from their crew's natural passion for the task at hand.

These units take great pride in how they maintain their craft and their equipment, and in every job they do. Other squadrons are professional, but their traditions of focusing on the details are not as strong. They do not generate the same drive and passion as the top squadrons. Still others suffer poor performance that brings down the whole group and requires real leadership to help them break through those negative cycles.

To be an organization that people recognize as being the best, you must create a culture of excellence from the very beginning, one that balances The Performance Triad and adds in the Performance Multiplier Effect.

Throughout this book we have discussed the important relationship of three key elements of The Performance Triad – passion, free will and focus. In the fire triangle of fuel, oxygen and heat, if you take away any one element, the fire goes out.

The performance triangle is the same. Take away any one of the three critical elements and the performance will fade. Organizations that focus on building a culture that promotes and balances the three elements of The Performance Triad will experience an incredible phenomenon that will give them the edge over their competition – the Performance Multiplier Effect.

Passion: The Oxygen

Passion is the fuel for the team. It puts life into the team, making them more cohesive and alive. Passion draws more people to want to become part of your team or support your team in some way. Business can take off from there. The Performance Multiplier Effect combined with the passion it engenders becomes a powerful, mutually reinforcing feedback loop.

Free Will: The Fuel

Free will is the oxygen that allows the team to breath. It provides momentum by allowing members of your team to harness their energy for the common good. Free will is where trust shines through – you trust that your training has worked, trust that your employees know what their goal is, and trust that their passion and their focus and mission-type orders will drive them across the finish line in the most effective way.

Focus: The Heat

Focus is the heat that helps set your coworkers' passion and free will ablaze. It generates a concentrated energy that pushes everyone in the organization forward. With properly aligned focus, every ounce of passion and free will are in use, no effort is wasted on the road to the goal.

The Business of the Triad Balance

Although there are plenty of good examples of the Performance Multiplier Effect in the military, some of the most remarkable examples exist in business, where entrepreneurs take a vision and build whole new enterprises that blow away the competition.

Southwest Airlines® is a good example. A 1971 startup, the company worked to forge a partnership with its employees to deliver passion to its customers. In fact, employees are identified as one of the groups of customers that the company serves.

Individuals also have a lot of flexibility in how they use their free will to solve problems. For example, flight attendants are given a list of rules that they must read to passengers before every flight, but they are left to their own free will to creatively deliver those rules. Only on Southwest will you find your FAA rules sung to you.

For the most part, even as Southwest Airlines has grown, it has kept its employees focused on their goal of delivering beyond-federally mandated service and quality to all of its customers. From flight attendants to the predictable pricing system to the standard-sizes of its fleet, Southwest does everything differently than its competition.

As a result, from its humble beginnings, Southwest has grown into one of the top airlines in the United States – and one of the few to be consistently profitable.

People Magnets

No matter how high the standards or how rigorous the application process, the best organizations I have observed from Southwest Airlines to the Blue Angels are personnel magnets.

Everyone wants to be a part of an organization with a unique quality, a balanced Performance Triad and the prestige that comes with it.

Even the Navy SEALs, which requires that applicants have incredible physical endurance just to make the team, draws hundreds of applicants per opening. It is this same type of mystique that inspires people to work 80 hours a week for little or no money at a start-up company with a clear mission to "change the world."

By building a culture that has a unique characteristic that sets it apart, and then applies techniques that encourage a harmonized Performance Triad, you will witness the same Performance Multiplier Effect in your organization.

Make the Magic Last

The Blue Angels has delivered a remarkable record of superior results for more than 60 years. TOPGUN has been producing the best fighter pilots in the world since 1968. These are no one-hit wonders.

This book focuses on the recipe – the combination of cultural habits and values – that enables the best organizations, like the Blue Angels and TOPGUN, to sustain the highest levels of performance year after year by leveraging passion, free will and focus.

This differentiator helps them to withstand the challenges they must overcome to stay on top: Changes in leadership and operating environments, unforeseen catastrophic events, and competitors' ever-present desire to knock them off.

The unique ingredients – embodied in cultural behaviors across the organization – are why some F/A-18 squadrons routinely score better in the Navy's Battle Efficiency competition, even though all the squadrons are given equal numbers of aircraft, spare parts, personnel, and operating budgets.

It is why iconic sports teams have more championship wins and consistent performance than their peers and why some rock bands continue to produce great music over many decades, while other bands fade away.

Remember, the goal of this book is to help you understand prescribed techniques of sustained performance and continuous improvement, embodied in a culture of excellence and created through passion, free will and focus. The experiences of the Blue Angels, TOPGUN and Naval Aviation is a starting point, a laboratory if you will, in which you can clearly see what works and what does not.

A lot of concepts contribute to the culture of excellence and we have simplified them here with concept of The Performance Triad.

It is especially important to understand a unique attribute of the Triad. Quite simply, a well-harmonized and balanced triad becomes a *performance multiplier* much like in military parlance, combining arms synergistically with maneuver can become a *force multiplier.*

While you cannot reduce the multiplier effect to mathematical simplicity, the point is that an optimized triad is a game changer. In the right situation, it can produce order-of-magnitude improvements in outcomes.

<u>Harmonized Triad → Performance Multiplier Effect → Consistently Better Execution in All Areas Leading to Mission Success!</u>

The results can be spectacular.

When I was a Carrier Air Wing Commander with seven squadrons working directly for me, I could see the difference culture made each time I flew with each one. Those with the best cultures always had more passion, focus and innovation when executing their missions. Their level of enthusiasm when you walked into the ready-room was noticeably higher.

Much like a modern automobile engine with computerized ignition and fuel injection systems that are continuously working to optimize themselves to produce the most power for the least amount of fuel, organizations with cultures that continuously optimizes the Triad get the most from their resources.

Points to Remember

1. Balancing passion, free will and focus among your staff and coworkers will create the Performance Multiplier Effect, at which point you will see a dramatic improvement in performance within your organization.

2. High standards and a rigorous work ethic will attract more like-minded employees and improve

the quality of your new and current employees. The key is to be consistent in your standards all the way down to the smallest detail.

3. Continuous improvement at all levels of an organization will enhance your stature and propel your organization to new heights.

Visualization

Envision your hiring process. What are the steps you take to identify new employees? Do you have to go looking for them, or do you have a wait list? Do you consider unsolicited applicants, or do you rely on job descriptions and computerized applications? What mechanism do you have to evaluate passion, free will and focus of potential employees or coworkers?

Visualize your ideal system for finding quality employees. When visualizing this perfect system, do not worry about the time or money involved to make it come true. Does this system involve developing a "farm team" or a group of people you would like to have but they need an additional skill or some more field experience? What are some ways you can do this – quarterly informational meetings, annual fair with contests that test skills, or monthly "pitch fests" where anyone can come tell you what they can do for you and you give feedback? If these ideas, or others that you have, seem to be costly in time and/or money, what can you do to shave off some costs? How can you get your organization to respect, embrace and participate in really getting to know and vet the candidates? How can you empower your team in a way that naturally attracts the best to your organization? Visualize the best knocking on your door, coming to you!

Brainstorm some ideas for identifying and measuring the passion, free will and focus of existing and potential employees. Do you have a lot of ideas in one of the three legs of the Triad? Not enough in another? Is this reflected in the talents of your existing staff? If so, how can you improve the other ingredients of your Triad – add more passion, encourage more use of free will, improve focus?

"The lasting value of a winning culture applies to any size organization, country or small team."

U.S. Navy Photo Taken By MC1 Mark O'Donald

Chapter 11:
The Lasting Value of a Winning Culture

"Glad to Be Here, Sir."

It was a Friday afternoon, just before a practice, and I was running outside the gates of Andrews Air Force Base, which is outside of Washington, DC, across the Maryland state line. As with a lot of our military bases, it was surrounded by many neighborhoods.

As I ran along the road, a high school boy who was obviously skipping school with his buddies started to run alongside me. He was joking and showing off to his friends. I challenged him to keep up with me, and slowly sped up until he could no longer keep pace.

I turned back, slowed down and invited him to the show the next day. Part of the Blues' culture is to always rise to a challenge – no matter how small – and to always be a good role model.

The following day, with all of the uneasy confidence of a teenager, the young man stood along the crowd line where I signed a poster for him. I was glad to see him again, though it would be the last time — his presence at the show told me that our brief encounter had made a lasting impression.

Encounters like this remind us how lucky we are, not just lucky to be Blue Angels, but lucky to have the opportunity to follow our passion, use our free will, and focus on what is important to us.

Not only do you owe it to your teammates to be your best and to develop a culture of excellence, but you owe it to the larger world around you. It is a sense of pride and inclusion that you carry with you, and share with everyone you meet. In other words, a culture of excellence stays with those who live it, well beyond their time in that organization. We carry it with us in all that we do.

Over the course of my career, many people have influenced me. I fondly recall the guys in my first squadron and my TOPGUN experience. I learned a great deal from those that came before me at the Blue Angels, the "Gray Beards" as we called them. I owe them a lot.

All these people have one thing in common: They cared about making sure that my peers and I were successful. It was a measure of their own success. In addition, my peers and I, though we were in competition with one another, made sure we supported one another and regularly strove to make one another better. We needed to be ready to cover one another's backs when we went into combat.

In my consulting business, I see this focus on watching each other's backs only in the very best organizations. The idea is that if we are all good, we will all achieve rewards together.

The people who have helped me in my career all promoted professionalism, a strong work ethic, a questioning attitude, continuous improvement, career advancement and ongoing education.

I will never forget what a joy it was for me, as a Blue Angel, to give rides to my first commanding officer and executive officer in a practice demo, 17 years after I started my career path. They were then a four-star and a three-star admiral, respectively. The experience was a fitting capstone to my professional development at that time. Seventeen years after I'd joined their squadron and learned from them, things had come full-circle.

It felt like I was thanking them for giving me such a great start, because it had worked: Here I was, giving them a ride in a Blue Angel F/A-18!

Portable Performance Triads

Take a look at the best organizations and the individuals who come from them. These organizations produce more winners – individuals who go on to produce great results in their careers – than other organizations.

Nearly every person who remained in the service from my first squadron went on to command at the highest levels in the Navy. That is certainly not true of many other squadrons.

The squadrons that have built great cultures of excellence produce more leaders and people who become successful than other squadrons. It is not so much that the individuals themselves are so much better. Rather, the organization has taught the team members how to accomplish things at a higher level and about how to develop and sustain a culture of excellence. That person then brings these best practices to any organization they join.

These leaders improve all the organizations with which they are affiliated and function not as caretakers but as Relentless Innovators.

Organizational leaders who understand the importance of developing the next generation and creating spirited competition avoid the zero-sum mentality. The idea that one individual's success comes at the expense of another is destructive and counter to how the United States, using free enterprise, came to have the highest standard of living in the world.

Our Founding Fathers knew that "equal opportunity" would not guarantee equal success or equal outcomes in terms of wealth or happiness. It would instead elevate the wealth and happiness of the entire country because we have equal opportunity to follow our own path.

Organizations with a culture of excellence offer a similar opportunity. They provide an environment to ensure everyone is rewarded for helping the entire organization become successful. They allow all team members an opportunity for a seat at the table.

Cultures of excellence give people a piece of the equity or a stake in the organization's outcome, but also requires each person take part in the risk of success or failure. When everyone puts skin in the game, it means, "We're all in this together, so let's go."

In the best companies I've seen, where people are truly all in it together, there's a shared risk but also a shared reward. This gives people a sense of ownership and works to elevate the entire organization to higher standards on all levels.

Looking Outside the Gates

Cultures of excellence expand their reach by sharing externally.

"Cultures of excellence make a habit of giving, as they always get more back in return."

Photo By Trent Kalp ©

From a commercial standpoint, the Blue Angels advances recruiting by exposing as many people in the country to the military in as positive a way as is possible. In the case of the Blues, it is in their best interest to go out and promote what they do.

For business, sports teams, or other organizations, the more they give back to the communities they impact, the more successful they become. Internally, it helps team members generate a sense of pride in their accomplishments. Externally, it helps because people see your organization in a more positive light because you are going out of your way to share.

I have many wonderful memories from when I was a Blue Angel, but the best of these relate to how deeply we Blues appreciated our audiences. In particular, we made a point of working with the Make-a-Wish® foundation, which helps kids facing serious, life-threatening illnesses.

Every Friday, for practice shows, we would have a Make-a-Wish group in our audience. For a practice show, we were frequently on a new, unfamiliar show site. We would be working to get used to everything that was new, typically one of the hardest things for us.

However, we would always make sure to sign autographs for the Make-a-Wish kids.

These children, often so attentive to our show and appreciative of the opportunity to be there, reinforced the whole point of our mission. We could really make a difference for them by letting them share in a thrilling performance and then answering each and every one of their questions.

The Make-a-Wish kids' great outlook on life always reminded me to be thankful for what I have and for the opportunity to do something that brings them joy.

Growing a Future With Purpose

Building a culture of excellence takes time, yet it can be destroyed in an instant if core values are lost. Those that are sustained over time have a clear purpose and keep the team on task to soundly think about decisions, keep up with changes, and roll with developments. Timing and tempo are crucial for continued success.

Instead of trying to fly lower and faster because it is late in the season and you want to push limits and put on a more spectacular show, remember the things that got you to where you are today. When you start to forget your history and your past battle lessons, things start unraveling.

Slower is often faster.

Maintaining tradition keeps current those core values that got you to where you are today. Traditions are a reminder of what made you successful, all the little things, all the basics, such as Coach Wooden saying every year to his new team, "Okay, here's how to tie your shoes."

Knowing the basics adds up to wins.

Cultures of Excellence Make the Difficult Look Easy

"We are having a little bit of fun on our traditional post-flight walk back at the end of the season. This marks the finish of a two-year tour for many of us. Cultures of excellence stay focused on the task at hand to the very end."

Photo by Toru EBISAWA ©

My very first lesson when I became the new Boss was learning how to perform the *Walkdown, Aircraft Startup Sequence and the Walkback*. When I arrived as the new Boss, I had seen the previous team's six demonstration pilots perform the Walkdown and Aircraft Startup Sequence numerous times.

The way the maintenance team prepared the aircraft, and the ease with which the pilots walked down, climbed up, strapped in and started the jet engines all in unison looked to me as though it would be easy to learn. I was wrong.

Keep in mind that at this point in my career I had thousands of flight hours and had manned up and started jet aircraft nearly as many times — but not the Blue Angels way. The effort needed to execute the choreographed actions smoothly took hours of practice until it was passable and in fact, this "simple" execution was critiqued in the same manner as all our most difficult airborne maneuvers in the debrief after every time we flew.

When you visualize all the moving elements that have to be perfectly synchronized, including marching in formation in front of a crowd of thousands of spectators, peeling off smartly one by one as each pilot reaches his jet and climbing quickly up the boarding ladder and into the cockpit, strapping in and starting the aircraft, all in unison, you can begin to see all the things that can go wrong. Each element had small details, not noticeable to the crowd, that could not be overlooked by us if we wanted to ensure everything looked precise.

Over time, I learned that it was the passion and focus we had as a team in putting attention into these small, seemingly unimportant details that made the performance look smooth and easy to a casual observer.

Whether your profession calls for strapping into a supersonic fighter jet with tens of thousands of pounds of thrust, piloting a Formula One race car through the tightest, high-speed corners, launching into space then having to come back to Earth—or something a little more conventional like selling a superior cup of coffee through thousands of retail stores, or pumping out hit computer products—the best teams have the passion to strive for perfection and efficiency in everything they do.

> *Teams get it right when they create a culture built around continuous improvement, maximum performance, and an unswerving focus on executing every aspect of their chosen field better than anyone else.*

A trademark of winning organizations is that they have a way of making the difficult look easy.

"The very first Blue Angel Team built a winning culture at the very beginning."

U.S. Navy Photo

Points to Remember

1. People who have had the privilege to be immersed in a culture of excellence will duplicate that culture in every organization they join, from that point forward. They focus on the details and take the pride with them wherever they go.

2. World-class organizations do not believe in the zero-sum game. They understand that improving each team member improves the whole team.

3. Top performers promote professionalism, a strong work ethic, a questioning attitude, continuous improvement, career advancement, and ongoing education.

4. When you are the best, you make it look easy.

Wrap-Up

I remember rolling out after landing and taxiing back from my last show as a Blue Angel.

We were pretty quiet on the way back to our parking spaces directly in front of the crowd of many thousands. You would think it would be a cause for celebration over the radio, but I did not want to say anything because we still had to shut down our airplanes and exit the cockpits without doing something dumb like falling down the ladders.

I wanted to stay focused and professional until the very end, until they had announced our names for the last time, until we had shaken hands at the crowd line for the last time. Only after that could we call it a wrap and relax.

At the end of our two-year assignment, we reviewed our strategic goals and whether we had achieved them. We felt a great sense of satisfaction at the end of the season.

- We had tightened up the show sequence as planned and elevated our media coverage.

- We had great reviews from the fans and fellow aviators.

- Even though we flew extremely close in a variety of environmental conditions, everybody still had their fingers and toes, nobody was hurt, and everything had gone well.

We were all smiling.

"Finishing a show season with all smiles. The winning legacy and culture of excellence continues."

U.S. Navy Photo

The picture of success is a perfectly executed mission that provides a launch pad for future perfectly executed missions.

From the Blue Angels, my fellow teammates and I went on to new milestones and different careers. As an individual, I brought the culture of excellence from the Blues and

TOPGUN into other organizations. I applied what I learned from the Blue Angels to everything else I did: My Carrier Air Wing, the Joint Chiefs in the Pentagon, NORAD, and NORTHCOM. I then brought what I learned from all of those organizations into my business.

If you focus only on winning, your organization will not be as effective because your mission parameters are too narrow. The very best organizations focus on world-class execution, not just on winning.

It is the culture that you must perfect, the ongoing culture that continually propels itself to new heights. Focus not on winning, but on creating a culture that will enable you to win. When you do that, you will build something truly special, something that lifts up and enables not just the organization itself and its team members but all who come in contact with it.

And, of course, always remember to maximize and balance your passion, free will and focus.

About the Author

Rob "Ice" Ffield's passion for participating in high-performance activities and building elite teams began in his teens when he excelled in several sports, including alpine ski racing and soccer. Leading as team captain in both disciplines, he accumulated numerous personal and team wins at state and regional competitions through to his college years.

His focus on innovation and the pursuit of perfection led to his unprecedented string of naval career milestones which included two tours as an air-combat instructor at the Navy's prestigious Navy Fighter Weapons School, TOPGUN; selection to lead the Navy Flight Demonstrations Squadron, the Blue Angels; and combat tours while in command of a strike fighter squadron and carrier air wing.

Rob capped his career by being hand-selected to lead the personal staffs for three and four-star generals in command at the highest levels of the military. He served as the Executive Officer for the Strategic Plans and Policy Directorate of the Joint Staff in the Pentagon and at North

American Aerospace Defense Command (NORAD) and U.S. Northern Command (NORTHCOM) in Colorado Springs as they crafted the "surge" plan for Iraq and made vast improvements to homeland defense.

Throughout his career, his relentless search for building winning strategies, tactics, and cultures led to numerous advances in air combat including his development and refinement of TOPGUN's night fighter tactics, which were critical to the Navy's Gulf War success. His research and lecturing on training excellence provided the initial inspiration for a core group of visionary fighter pilots and instructors who fundamentally reinvented TOPGUN's curriculum into the highly heralded program used today.

The combination of Rob's passion, free will and focus led to countless personal wins and also served to elevate the performance of every organization he joined. He won numerous air-to-air and air-to-ground combat competitions. When not winning outright, he always placed in the top one percent of the extremely competitive shipboard landing competitions spanning 25 years and nearly 1,000 aircraft carrier landings.

He was personally chosen early for the next rank three times throughout his career. His innovative spirit was a catalyst for execution excellence where he and his teammates won four Battle Efficiency Awards—a testament to their winning cultures.

Following his passion to focus on creating cultures of excellence, Rob left the Navy and founded the CATSHOT Group, named for the Navy's catapult shot that launches aircraft from aircraft carriers.

CATSHOT Group's name is symbolic of the company's goal of assisting elite teams by rapidly building the winning combination of passion, free will and focus necessary to succeed in launching and sustaining their business campaigns. Since its inception, CATSHOT Group has done just that with multi-billion-dollar organizations in the energy, aerospace and defense industries. They are currently expanding into other fields where performance matters.

Passionate about giving back, Rob co-founded CATSHOT Education Group, CATSHOT Veterans Education Group and Veterans Transition Inc. that are designed to provide executive-level business training to high-ranking military veterans. The programs focus on giving veterans the tools to be exceptional entrepreneurs.

Rob is married to his lovely wife, Mona, who is equally passionate, free-willed and focused in her career as a U.S. Air Force officer and jet pilot. Rob's three grown daughters are successfully pursuing their own careers in art, international relations and medicine.

Connect with Rob on LinkedIn:
www.linkedin.com/pub/rob-ffield/9/255/585

Or visit his website for more information:

www.catshotgroup.com

Glossary of Terms

A

Air Boss — Highly experienced Naval aviator who controls flight operations within 10 miles of the aircraft carrier. Includes all launches and recovery operations on the flight deck.

AGL — An aviation acronym that stands for Above Ground Level. It is measured in feet.

B

Blue Angels — The traditional name of the Navy Flight Demonstration Squadron.

Boss — The commanding officer and flight leader of the Blue Angels. The Boss flies the jet signified with a number "1" on the tail.

C

Ceiling — The aviation term/measurement that gives the altitude in feet of the bottom of a cloud layer.

D

Demo — or "The Demo." The shortened version of the word "demonstration" that refers to the series of maneuvers that constitutes a Blue Angel air show.

Diamond — See Formations.

Diamond Pilots — The Blue Angels refer to numbers "1" through "4" as the "Diamond" or "Diamond Pilots."

Dirty Configuration — An aircraft is considered "dirty" when the landing gear is extended while the aircraft is flying. The Blue Angels perform a looping maneuver with the landing gear in the extended position. It is called the Diamond Dirty Loop.

Double Farvel — The Blue Angel Diamond Formation where the Boss and Slot pilot are inverted.

F

Fat Albert — The nickname given to the Blue Angel C-130 that is used to transport all support personnel and gear and also to perform a high-performance air show that demonstrates maneuvers used by the United States Marine Corps in combat situations.

Flight Deck Personnel — All personnel that work on the flight deck wear specific color jerseys to signify their role.

Formations used by the Blue Angels:

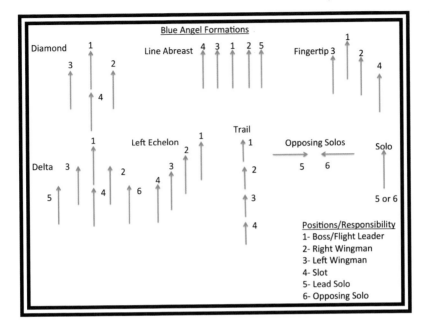

K

"Knock it Off" — A term used by any airborne or ground safety personnel to tell all involved to terminate an air show demonstration or practice due to safety concerns.

Knots — The shortened/slang version of nautical miles per hour. One knot is equal to 1.15 miles per hour.

L

Left Wingman — Flies on the left side of the Diamond Formations. The Left Wingman flies the jet signified with a number "3" on its tail. The Left Wingman is typically a pilot on his first year as a Blue Angel. Traditionally, number "3" moves to the Slot position (number "4") on his second year on the team. See Formations.

Left Echelon Roll — A signature Blue Angel maneuver where Blue Angels numbers "1" through "4" do a very precise rolling maneuver while in Left Echelon Formation. See Formations.

Line Abreast Loop — A looping maneuver conducted by Blue Angels "1" through "5" while in a Line Abreast Formation. See Formations.

M

Maintenance Master Chief — The senior enlisted chief petty officer who is in charge of orchestrating the effort of all aircraft maintenance operations and functions.

Mission Completion Rate — One of the formal metrics the Navy uses to grade how well a squadron performs. It is based on the number of sorties that are completed versus the number of sorties that were scheduled.

N

Nautical Miles per Hour — The measurement of speed used in aviation. One nautical mile per hour is equal to 1.15 miles per hour. "Knots" is a slang term referring to nautical miles per hour.

R

Right Wingman — The Right Wingman flies on the right side of the Blue Angel Diamond Formation. A number "2" on the tail signifies the right Wingman's jet. The Right

Wingman traditionally is a Marine Corps Officer and he remains in that position for both his first and second years on the team. See Formations.

S

Slot Pilot—The Slot pilot flies the jet with the number "4" on the tail and is positioned directly behind and below the Boss/number "1" jet. He acts as the airborne safety officer for all formation maneuvers due to his position and experience. The Slot pilot traditionally is the previous year's number 3. See Formations.

Solos—The Blue Angels refer to number "5" and number "6" as "The Solos" or the "Solo pilots." The Lead Solo pilot is on his second year as a demonstration pilot and was the previous year's number 6 Opposing Solo pilot.

T

TOPGUN—The name given to the organization known as the U.S. Navy Fighter Weapons School.

W

Walkdown—The term used to describe the formal start of the air show demonstration where the pilots march in front of their aircraft and one by one enter their cockpits.

Walkback—The term used to describe the formal ending of a Blue Angels air show when the pilots "1" through "6" climb out of their aircraft and march in formation to a position where they salute and shake hands.

Wingman — Naval Flight Formations are made up of a flight lead and wingman. The lead will lead and the wingman, or wingmen follow.

Index

See also Glossary of Terms beginning p. 203.